Working Together
in Schools

A Guide for Educators

Gordon A. Donaldson Jr.
David R. Sanderson

CORWIN PRESS, INC.
A Sage Publications Company
Thousand Oaks, California

For information address:

Corwin Press, Inc.
A Sage Publications Company
2455 Teller Road
Thousand Oaks, California 91320
E-mail: order@corwin.sagepub.com

SAGE Publications Ltd.
6 Bonhill Street
London EC2A 4PU
United Kingdom

SAGE Publications India Pvt. Ltd.
M-32 Market
Greater Kailash I
New Delhi 110 048 India

Printed in the United States of America

Library of Congress Cataloging-in-Publication Data

Donaldson, Gordon A., Jr.
    Working together in schools: A guide for educators / authors,
Gordon A. Donaldson, Jr., David R. Sanderson.
        p.   cm.
    Includes bibliographical references and index.
    ISBN 0-8039-6377-7 (cloth).—ISBN 0-8039-6378-5 (pbk.)
    1. Teaching teams—United States. 2. Teacher participation in
administration—United States. I. Sanderson, David R. II. Title.
LB1029.T4D66 1996
371.1'48—dc20   96-10087

98 99 10 9 8 7 6 5 4 3 2

Corwin Production Editor: Diana E. Axelsen
Corwin Typesetter: Andrea D. Swanson

Contents

Acknowledgments

The inspiration for this book germinated in our own working together with educators, around their working together. Because of Gordon's career in schools and David's in staff development and organizational consulting, we have found ourselves repeatedly helping teachers, administrators, counselors, students, and parents to work more closely and affirmatively with one another. Our own collaboration in the Maine Academy for School Leaders in 1992, nurtured by many years of friendship, led us to the decision to compose a book that would encourage and assist educators in this important endeavor. We have many people and experiences to thank for our own educations in working together. We each trace our learning about collaboration in schools to our earliest jobs as teachers. Over the years since then, we have learned from many, many people. Among them are Peter B. Rosenbaum, Dan Cheever, Donna D'Entremont, Tony Bok, Dick Barnes, Cynthia Donaldson, Roland Barth, Lucianne Carmichael, Anne Marie Read, David Brown, Becky van der Bogert, Richard Ackerman, David Bourns, Eileen Conlon, Michael Brazzel, Nancy Coverstone, Doug Babkirk, Aileen Fortune, Louise Franck Cyr, Bill Weber, Deb Burwell, Jim Killacy, Patricia Williams, and colleagues with the National Rural Development Institute. We thank particularly three friends and practitioner colleagues who provided thoughtful feedback on manuscripts: George Marnik and Beth Lyons, principal and teacher leader respectively at Mount Desert Island High School, Bar Harbor, Maine, and

Ron Beard, Extension Educator at the University of Maine. For her assistance with the cover design, we are grateful to Nell Donaldson, our talented artistic consultant. Our own collaboration for this book grew over numerous land-clearing and brush-burning outings on snowy afternoons, damp spring mornings, and crystal-blue summer days, all on the shores of Martin's Cove. The convergence of salt air, spruce smoke, gulls' chorus, and physical co-laboring played no small part in the cultivation of the ideas and the relationship that brought this book to fruition. For all of these we are grateful. Our own collaboration, we trust, will inspire yours.

About the Authors

Gordon A. Donaldson, Jr., is Professor of Education at the University of Maine and Coordinator of the Maine Network of School Leaders. He also consults with school systems on school improvement and team building. He has written about school leadership and has helped create new leadership development opportunities for educators since the mid-1970s. He is a cofounder of the Maine Principals' Academy, is a founding member of the International Network of Principals' Centers, and was Director of the Maine Academy for School Leaders.

Dr. Donaldson began his career in education as a teacher and principal in middle and high schools in several states in the Northeast. He has authored numerous articles and four other books: *Learning to Lead: The Dynamics of the High School Principalship* (1991); *Becoming Better Leaders: The Challenge of Improving Student Learning*, with George Marnik (1995); *As Leaders Learn: Personal Stories of Growth in School Leadership*, edited with George Marnik (1995); and *Making Sense as a School Leader: Persisting Questions, Creative Opportunities*, with Richard Ackerman and Rebecca van der Bogert (1996). He holds an A.B. degree from Harvard College and M.A.T. and Ed.D. degrees from the Harvard Graduate School of Education.

David R. Sanderson is an organizational consultant whose career in higher and secondary education has included college teaching, secondary school administration, and leadership in staff and organization development in the University of Maine Cooperative Extension. He has worked in the field of organization development since 1986 and specializes in organizational change, strategic planning, conflict and diversity management, and coalition building. His clients include schools and school districts, health care organizations, Native American tribes, colleges, university departments and divisions, and government agencies.

Dr. Sanderson is affiliated with the National Rural Development Institute at the University of Wisconsin, which is dedicated to building coalitions among organizations seeking innovative approaches to societal issues through collaboration. He has published a variety of scholarly papers and staff development materials. He is a member of the national Organization Development Network, the Maine chapter of the OD Network, and SearchNet, the national network of consultants who design and lead future search conferences. He holds a Ph.D. in English from the University of California at Davis.

An Invitation to Our Readers

We want to hear about your experience as you read our book and apply it to your practice as educators. We welcome your responses, feedback, and inquiries. You may contact us by phone, mail, or e-mail.

Gordon A. Donaldson, Jr.   David R. Sanderson
Professor of Education   Organizational Consultant
University of Maine   RFD #2, Eagle Point
Orono, ME 04469-5766   Ellsworth, ME 04605
207 581-2450   207 667-1213
gordond@maine.maine.edu   dsand@acadia.net

Teacher cultures, the relationships between teachers and their colleagues, are among the most educationally significant aspects of teachers' lives and work. . . . What goes on inside the teacher's classroom cannot be divorced from the relations that are forged outside it.

—Andy Hargreaves and Michael Fullan,
Understanding Teacher Development (1992)

Introduction

Why Work Together?

Wendy McClure shot to her feet, unable to contain her thoughts and feelings any longer. This silliness simply must stop, she thought; our students' ability levels are so varied that you have to be a dolt to think that you can successfully teach the whole range in one class!

"Wait just a minute here!" she exclaimed. Peg Stanley, who had been speaking to the assembled faculty, turned abruptly toward Wendy. Heads craned. For a few moments, silence dominated the room. "I've been at this business for 19 years now, and we've tried so many ways of individualizing and grouping, and none of them has worked. Let's face it, teaching all levels of kids at once is so cumbersome that we can't pull it off. Let's settle this once and for all. Homogeneous grouping is the only practical way to go!"

Wendy's interruption of the Sandford Elementary faculty's lively discussion of multilevel grouping pumped the anxiety level of the group up several notches. Peg Stanley, the principal, stood speechless. Teachers shifted in their seats; some coughed. Peter McCardy finally broke the silence. "I know what you mean, Wendy. I've been thinking the same thing. It feels to me like we're starting to go through what we've been through before, like it's time for the heterogeneous grouping shtick again. Personally, I'm for doing more for the lower kids, but I can't see that this new program will do it."

Sally Tannenbaum jumped to her feet, red-faced: "I've been here at Sandford for 4 years, and I've taught nothing but kids who're marginal. I've got mostly minority kids, they're all behind grade level, they're absent a lot, and when they're here they're pulled out for special ed and every other type of remedial help. I'm sick of it, and I'm upset with the tone of this discussion!"

"OK, OK, Sally," Peg burst in. "I know you're frustrated and you really want some change here, but Wendy has a point of view we need to consider, and so does Peter. Our discussions this spring have shown us some ways to go, and I think we'll get there eventually. But everyone's got a right to be heard, and we all need to get along with each other."

"But Peg," Sally rejoined, "this discussion is going the way all our discussions about change go. We study an idea for 4 months. We get close to the end of the year, and some of us push for a decision. And what happens? We don't make one. People always have too many objections or raise too many problems. We don't dare take the plunge. I'm sorry, but I think it's time we fish or cut bait around here!"

So it goes in school faculties, year in and year out. New programs, new goals and practices, and new people trickle into the mainstreams of school life. Some blend into the current, contributing to the dominant flow; others do not mix well with standard practice and are forced into backwaters and eddies at the margins; and still others never join the stream at all, as ideas and people simply leave the school. Change in schools involves the intermingling of delicate and tentative new ideas with a powerfully moving social, cultural, and behavioral stream.

Adults in schools both constitute and control much of that stream. Wendy, Peggy, Peter, Sally, and their colleagues shape the daily patterns of mind, heart, and body at Sandford Elementary. Sally is frustrated with a dynamic in her faculty that effectively curtails real change. Wendy has chosen a crucial end-of-the-year faculty meeting in which to raise her deepest doubts about the grouping proposal. Why did she not raise them earlier, when they could be dealt with? Peter seemingly throws his weight behind Wendy's objections, but he leaves the door open to future persuasion. And Principal Peg's intervention aims more at smoothing the emotional turmoil than at resolving the difficult question at hand.

Surely, if any change is to take hold in the many classrooms and activities of Sandford Elementary, it must be well understood, endorsed, and carried into practice by the adults in this room. So, too, in every other school. Reforming schools is, in large part, a matter of enlisting and empowering the people in them to reshape how they think, feel, and act (Barth, 1991; Fullan & Hargreaves, 1991). The long-term success of school improvement rides on the ability of adults to function productively together. Many recognize this need for greater collaboration and greater teamwork (Darling-Hammond, 1994; Lieberman, 1988). Yet many remain frustrated by their inability to change how they function together so they can experience greater success with each other and with their students.

We invite you, the reader, to explore with us a variety of forms for collaboration in schools. We suggest a framework for understanding how to build stronger working relationships with and among your colleagues as you together meet the challenges of serving children better. As we proceed, we offer you practical suggestions to enhance your experience of working together.

The Benefits of Working Together

Why work together? The question lies at the heart of any collection of adults who convene around a common goal. We will recommend throughout this book that you and your colleagues repeatedly ask and answer it. You will find that collaborating with others requires time, energy, and emotional investment. As with all investments, you cannot avoid wondering at some point, as Wendy McClure does, if the investment is worth it.

In our own moments of such reassessment, we find ourselves coming back to three basic arguments for collaboration. First, working together has *direct benefits for children*. As adults share information about students, teaching, and their roles as parents and teachers, their repertoires are enriched, and their effectiveness with their students and children grows. The idea of two adults sharing information about a child resounds with two-heads-are-better-than-one logic. Particularly as the education and upbringing of children have become more complex, the logic of bringing multiple resources to bear on tough teaching and learning problems seems compelling.

Indeed, studies by Newmann and Wehlage (1995), Johnson (1990), and Little (1982) provide evidence that closer teamwork on day-to-day pedagogical challenges promotes the improvement of teaching and brings benefits to students. Lieberman and Miller's (1991) review of teaching conditions and professional development also links collaboration to enriched teaching, learner-centered planning, and better learning. Linda Darling-Hammond (1993) and her colleagues have for years argued that teachers cannot improve their performance in isolation; they need caring colleagues to give second opinions, share ideas that work with students, and help sustain new practices with those students.

Second, working together has *direct benefits for educators.* As educators learn to work together, their sophistication and professional efficacy grow, contributing to a rising spiral in the quality of their work with one another and with children. Susan Rosenholtz's study of schools (1989) discovered that in what she called "moving" schools, teachers had more opportunity for collegial contact and that these contacts built norms of collaborative effort that made a difference in student achievement. Mirroring the findings of others such as Johnson (1990) and Schlechty (1990), Rosenholtz found that

> without common goals . . . teachers' instructional paths lead them in entirely disparate directions, each teacher compelled by her or his own pedagogical interests, each protected by school norms of self-reliance. Ironically, as teachers contemplate the enormous challenges before them, . . . perhaps the best weapon they could wield against uncertainty lies in colleagues, particularly teacher leaders, within their schools. (p. 69)

Contributors to Anne Lieberman's *Building a Professional Culture in Schools* (1988) draw from a variety of research efforts to assert that common goals, collegiality, a problem-solving orientation, membership in a professional group that focuses on the improvement of practice, and the exercise of teacher leadership all contribute to enhanced morale and performance. In the words of Patricia Wasley (1991), "Studies indicate that teacher growth and change thrive in an environment where the school community shares values and goals, where teachers are provided the time to reflect and to work together, where people are taught to work collaboratively, and where they are focused on issues of curriculum and instruction" (p. 20).

The third major benefit of collaboration is the *professional enrichment of the school's culture.* Practically every major education writer currently argues that school improvement is obstructed by hierarchical structure, bureaucracy, union-management hostilities, and overregulation. Many, such as Thomas Sergiovanni (1994), Seymour Sarason (1991), Thomas Toch (1991), and Philip Schlechty (1990), further assert that schools can move forward only if decision-making authority and strategic autonomy are collectively held by those closest to students: teachers and parents. Roland Barth's influential 1990 book *Improving Schools From Within* demonstrates how adults working in open "communities of learners" can create a new culture in schools that gives every child and every adult a legitimate place in the school and its governance.

Shedd and Bacharach (1991) concluded from their study of teachers and restructuring that the culture in schools needs nothing short of new norms:

> Schools that couple a "norm of continuous development" with a "norm of collegiality," making skill development and school improvement collective rather than merely individual imperatives, can tap each teacher's natural interest and personal growth and generate a receptivity to innovation and change. Schools in which teachers remain isolated—and insulated—from each other and from administrators encourage the opposite orientation. (pp. 100-101)

Despite an absence of extensive empirical support, these claims enjoy widespread support in practitioner and policy communities and are reinforced by thinker-practitioners working primarily in the corporate world (Senge, 1990; Weisbord, 1987; Wheatley, 1992).

These three major arguments for collaboration—that they will benefit children, educators, and the culture of the school—are often intertwined in studies and rhetoric. Indeed, we know of few who would argue against more productive working relationships among adults in schools. The difficult question is, How will these relationships grow? Although schools nearly unanimously support collaboration as a concept, they still struggle to create the conditions and the relationships that will encourage and sustain collaboration.

The Plan of Our Book

Our guiding principle as we wrote this book was "Make it useful and usable to busy educators and school staff." We start each chapter as we did this introduction, with a scenario from our experience that illustrates an opportunity to collaborate—and the difficulties inherent in these opportunities in busy schools. Calling on David's background in organization development and Gordon's study of schools, we then frame some suggestions for teachers, principals, counselors, and support staff to use as they strive to enhance their work together to benefit their students. Although our book is directed at school staffs, we hope parents, PTA groups, school board members, and central office personnel will find it helpful in their own work and, just as important, in their appreciation of the vital roles they play in supporting collaboration among faculty and staff. Although we had hoped to address more directly this wider array of participants in collaboration, space requirements precluded our doing so here.

We envision you, our readers, reading and discussing this book together with colleagues at school. Though it is not a manual on group process, it informs and reminds you about essential matters in the formation and development of the pairs and groups in which you are working. By together reading a chapter relevant to your form of collaboration, you can put our ideas directly to work.

We have kept our tone informal in the hope that you and your teammates will find it easy to engage with us in the book. In each chapter, we have inserted in boxes synopses of often-used techniques, sample agendas, and reminders that we felt you would find especially practical (the information in these boxes is often applicable to *all* chapters, so feel free to photocopy them). The following overview of chapters should help you select from the book those chapters that suit your own needs as a pair or group. (Although we urge you to start with Chapter 1 and end with Chapter 9, our book does not have to be read from front to back.)

Chapter 1 establishes the groundwork for our thinking about collaboration in two respects. First, we present our basic understanding of collaborative relationships and a straightforward model for understanding the process of collaboration. Then we introduce the "bedrock skills" of listening and influencing that you and your colleagues will need as you work together.

In Chapters 2 through 8, we address seven common opportunities for adults to work together in schools: two ways of pairing up with another educator, four types of small group work, and one type of working with the faculty as a whole. The bulk of each chapter is devoted to ideas and strategies for forming and fostering effective work relationships. We organize these ideas and strategies according to the four phases of collaboration in our process model:

- *Convening:* establishing purpose and membership
- *Contracting:* creating mission and the group
- *Composing:* designing collaborative action
- *Following through:* taking action and attaining closure

Each of these chapters closes with a list of conditions essential for collaboration in schools and an annotated list of resources for further reading.

Chapter 9 presents several overarching recommendations for nurturing collaboration in schools, based on the preceding chapters. First, we examine some of the common obstacles that educators face: a school culture that does not value or understand collaborative work, conflict within and outside the group, and flagging energy and commitment. We close with recommendations about four critical facilitating conditions for collaboration: space, time, leadership, and a supportive culture.

References

Barth, R. (1991). *Improving schools from within.* San Francisco: Jossey-Bass.

Darling-Hammond, L. (Ed.). (1993). *Professional development schools: Schools for developing a profession.* New York: Teachers College Press.

Darling-Hammond, L. (1994). *The current status of teaching and teacher development in the United States: Background paper prepared for the National Commission on Teaching and America's Future.* New York: Teachers College, Columbia University.

Fullan, M., & Hargreaves, A. (1991). *What's worth fighting for: Working together for your school.* Andover, MA: Regional Laboratory for the Educational Improvement of the Northeast and Islands.

Johnson, S. M. (1990). *Teachers at work: Achieving success in our schools.* New York: Basic Books.

Lieberman, A. (Ed.). (1988). *Building a professional culture in schools.* New York: Teachers College Press.

Lieberman, A., & Miller, L. (1991). *Staff development in education in the '90s: New demands, new realities, new perspectives.* New York: Teachers College Press.

Little, J. W. (1982). Norms of collegiality and experimentation. *American Educational Research Journal, 19,* 329-338.

Newmann, F., & Wehlage, G. (1995). *Successful school restructuring: A report to the public and educators.* Madison: University of Wisconsin, Center on Organization and Restructuring of Schools.

Rosenholtz, S. (1989). *Teachers' workplace: The social organization of schools.* New York: Longman.

Sarason, S. (1991). *The predictable failure of educational reform: Can we change course before it's too late?* San Francisco: Jossey-Bass.

Schlechty, P. (1990). *Schools for the 21st century: Leadership imperatives for educational reform.* San Francisco: Jossey-Bass.

Senge, P., Kleiner, A., Roberts, C., Ross, R. B., & Smith, B. J. (1994). *The fifth discipline fieldbook: Strategies and tools for building a learning organization.* New York: Doubleday.

Sergiovanni, T. (1994). *Building community in schools.* San Francisco: Jossey-Bass.

Shedd, J., & Bacharach, S. (1991). *Tangled hierarchies: Teachers as professionals and the management of schools.* San Francisco: Jossey-Bass.

Toch, T. (1991). *In the name of excellence: The struggle to reform the nation's schools, why it's failing, and what must be done.* New York: Oxford University Press.

Wasley, P. (1991). *Teachers who lead.* New York: Teachers College Press.

Weisbord, M. R. (1987). *Productive workplaces: Organizing and managing for dignity, meaning, and community.* San Francisco: Jossey-Bass.

Wheatley, M. (1992). *Leadership and the new science.* San Francisco: Berrett-Koehler.

1

Collaboration

The Heart of Working Together

Collaborative work, though complex, has two fundamental components: a respectful relationship among the collaborators and a productive process that assists the collaborators to do their work. In this chapter, we introduce these two essentials so you can understand how we weave them into successive chapters. We also introduce some "bedrock" skills that individuals use as they work productively together.

Collaboration Requires a Relationship

When two or more people work together effectively, their professional relationship is a foundation for that work. That relationship is affected by each individual's understanding of the other person or people, their motives for being there, their abilities, and their trustworthiness. In schools, we often pay too little attention to this relationship, sometimes assigning people to work together without asking if their professional relationship is strong enough to make collaboration work.

As we explore the opportunities adults have to work together in schools, we will return frequently to the matter of relationships. Each time we do, we will hark back to three attributes of a collaborative relationship. First, the partners in the relationship have developed a *fundamental commitment* to work with one another. The array of adults in schools is wide and colorful: teachers of various grades, subjects, and types of children; administrators; counselors; parents; secretaries; custodians; coaches; school board members; and PTA officers. Yet these people can collaborate effectively to make their joint effort greater than the sum of their individual efforts when they feel a common commitment.

Second, in collaborative relationships, people *understand one another's talents and accept one another's foibles.* Working together means pooling intellectual, material, and emotional resources. As a pair or a group solves individual and organizational problems, its success lies in the superiority of that solution to the solutions individuals could have generated. The relationship between or among collaborators can bring an advantage to them largely because those collaborators recognize how their talents can best be merged to compensate for their individual shortcomings. Once again, the relationship itself must be strong enough to permit individual differences to surface, be recognized, and be harnessed for the good of the group.

Third, relationships that sustain collaborative work are characterized by *respect and trust.* Very few relationships are free of conflict, whether in the form of personal habits that grate on us or of open, lengthy debates because our philosophies are different. As Benjamin Franklin (1945) put it at the final session of the Constitutional Convention in 1787, "When you assemble a number of individuals to have the advantage of their joint wisdom, you inevitably assemble with them all their prejudices, their passions, their errors of opinion, their local interests and their selfish views. From such an assembly can a perfect production be expected?" (p. 354). In collaborative relationships, people put themselves at least figuratively in the hands of their partners. Respect for one another's opinions and motives and trust in one another's judgment make this possible.

A Process Framework for Working Together

Over the years, researchers and organizational thinkers have explored patterns in the workplace, seeking to understand how productivity is shaped by the organization of work and workers. From this literature, we have learned not only that teams can be extraordinarily productive (Lawler, 1986; Weisbord, 1987) but also that effective working relationships can be characterized by patterns (Latzko, 1995; Senge, 1990; Wheatley, 1992). Movements to restructure work environments, such as the Total Quality Management and Quality Circles efforts, often try to put these patterns in place where they did not exist before.

We have drawn from the literature on productivity, teams, and group dynamics a framework to describe the general process of working together. This framework parallels other models, but we apply it to any and all collaborative work situations: situations in which two or more people come together to accomplish a task. We have found it helpful both as a checklist of reminders as pairs and groups form and move into a full collaboration and as a diagnostic blueprint to assess how a group is working. Each of our major chapters is organized around the four phases in the framework.

The four phases overlie nine activities that collaborators typically engage in. We suggest that you keep in mind the *progression* of the phases and activities as you think about the diagram in Box.1.1.

We present this framework with one major caution: As with all process models, it tends to oversimplify what happens under real working conditions. Collaboration seldom occurs in the clean, linear fashion that this list of nine progressive steps implies. Instead, a pair or group of adults will often be engaged in several of the nine activities at once. For example, groups often continue recruiting new members while the contracting of mission, goals, and ground rules is going on. Similarly, the best strategies and action plans (Steps 5 and 6) are often the result of trial runs at taking action (Step 8). We encourage you to think of this as a general framework of important activities that typify successful working pairs and groups.

Bedrock Skills for Collaboration

Throughout the book, we return repeatedly to two categories of skills we call "bedrock skills." As you collaborate, you draw repeatedly on these skills to help you succeed. Like the bedrock we walk on every day, they support the substantive work of a pair or group and sustain the relationships that collaboration needs. The two sets of skills are *listening* and *influencing* (see Box 1.2).

Listening Skills

Listening or attending skills form the essential basis for any interaction, from a consultative pair discussion to a large faculty meeting. Paying careful attention, striving to understand, helping to clarify—these are the first vital ways in which individuals contribute to a pair or group. Listening skills have special value for drawing out

Box 1.1

Framework for the
Process of Working Together

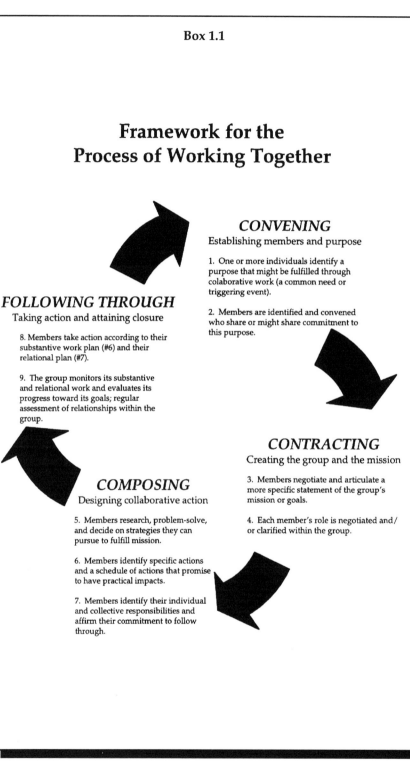

CONVENING
Establishing members and purpose

1. One or more individuals identify a purpose that might be fulfilled through colaborative work (a common need or triggering event).

2. Members are identified and convened who share or might share commitment to this purpose.

FOLLOWING THROUGH
Taking action and attaining closure

8. Members take action according to their substantive work plan (#6) and their relational plan (#7).

9. The group monitors its substantive and relational work and evaluates its progress toward its goals; regular assessment of relationships within the group.

CONTRACTING
Creating the group and the mission

3. Members negotiate and articulate a more specific statement of the group's mission or goals.

4. Each member's role is negotiated and/or clarified within the group.

COMPOSING
Designing collaborative action

5. Members research, problem-solve, and decide on strategies they can pursue to fulfill mission.

6. Members identify specific actions and a schedule of actions that promise to have practical impacts.

7. Members identify their individual and collective responsibilities and affirm their commitment to follow through.

and clarifying each person's ideas, goals, and values. By attending to others, we honor them, and we feel honored when they attend to us. Throughout the book, we emphasize the four listening skills described below.

> **Box 1.2**
> **The Bedrock Skills**
>
> Listening Skills
> - Being present
> - Interviewing
> - Reflecting
> - Summarizing
>
> Influencing Skills
> - Identifying intervention points
> - Using straight talk
> - Giving feedback

Being Present

Chances are you have demonstrated many times the basic behavior that shows you are present with and interested in another person. It may seem natural, for instance, to look at others when they are speaking to you individually or in a meeting. The skills of showing that "you are there" in all senses of the term rest, first, on a prior decision you make—an act of will in which you consciously decide to *pay attention,* to be with the other person or the group in that moment. A crucial dimension of that decision involves taking a nonjudgmental stance or attitude. "Being with" others suggests trying to understand them rather than evaluating their opinions, suggestions, and behavior.

Being present also means *demonstrating* your interest in others, encouraging them to express themselves honestly, without the "editing" that comes when they worry about your reaction. Encouraging involves giving cues that say, "I'm interested in you, your ideas, and your feelings—no matter what." Some cues are verbal ("uh-huh," "I see"). Many are nonverbal facial expressions and small gestures we make in response to what we hear (turning to face your partner, leaning toward a person speaking in a meeting). Even being attentively silent, particularly after you have asked a question, can act as a powerful encouragement to others.

Others rely on these attending behaviors to feel included and respected. Small as they are, it is still almost impossible to overstate their importance for building trust and encouraging others' active participation and full involvement.

Interviewing

The skill of interviewing arises from the decision to "look into" another's ideas, feelings, and concerns, mutually exploring his or her point of view to see what lies behind it. Interviewing requires two things. The first is to set aside your preferences, answers, and advice for the other person so that you—and he or she—can better understand what the person values and means. The second is to ask questions well to uncover what the other person thinks and feels. Interviewing skills stress using open-ended questions to encourage expansive answers— for example, "What seemed to cause the friction you noticed?" "How are you feeling about what happened next?" or "How are you understanding his behavior at this point?" A series of such questions can reveal many facets of a situation so both of you or the group can address it in an informed manner.

Reflecting

Perhaps the most sophisticated listening skill, *reflecting* involves restating what you have just heard and checking to see whether your restatement is accurate. A useful reflection has these qualities and effects:

- It is not burdened by your own opinion, evaluation, or theory about what you have heard.
- It is cast in your own words (thus not parroting the other person), yet it captures his or her meaning without distortion.
- It captures the essence (not all the details) of what has been communicated, including all major aspects of what you have heard, and offers them back in a shortened form.
- It elicits a response such as "Yes," "Exactly!" or even "Well, not exactly . . ." (with further clarification of a point). A reflection should be largely accurate, but it need not be completely so.

The art of reflecting comes from concentrating on all that you are observing, selecting what to reflect back, and then restating what you have heard. Concluding with a slight hesitancy or a direct question— "Does that sound right?"—offers your colleague the opportunity to confirm your reflection or revise it for greater accuracy.

Summarizing

Summaries have great power at key points in meetings and conversations. A summary is especially useful after a long discussion and near the end of a meeting. You might also begin a subsequent meeting with a summary as a way of focusing attention and preparing for further work.

To summarize a discussion, cast back over all or part of the conversation, gather the major points, and present them to the other person or group as briefly as possible. You are trying to "hear for the group" by collecting contributions from a complex, perhaps meandering conversation and putting them before the group again for another hearing. A summary is most effective if it ends tentatively, with a request for confirmation ("Is that what you meant?" or "Is that a fair summary?").

Influencing Skills

The second aspect of communication, *influencing skills,* involves our ability to speak for ourselves, say where we stand, and disclose otherwise hidden currents of thought and feeling. For strong relationships, whether with one other person or a group of people, the receptivity of listening is necessary but not sufficient. Influencing skills give us an effective voice so we can assert ourselves as well as listen.

Whereas listening skills require an awareness of yourself and of the person or people to whom you are listening, influencing skills require an additional awareness of the interpersonal process occurring between or among you. As you assert yourself to influence what is happening in your group, you need to be able to "read" how best to do this so that your effect is what you desire. The bedrock influencing skills are identifying intervention points, using straight talk, and giving feedback.

Identifying Intervention Points

The first influencing skill involves watching the progress of interactions in a pair or group as you take part in it. It is the skill of identifying when, in that progress, it would be helpful to make a contribution. As you use this skill, you draw on your knowledge of how human interaction proceeds, what can derail or stall it, and how it can be facilitated.

Every interaction, whether in a pair or group, works in two interwoven dimensions—the relationships among the members and the tasks they perform—much like the warp and woof of threads on a loom. We return to the image of a loom at several points in our book because it often captures in a simple image the complex interaction of forces at work in a pair or group. In this instance, the warp represents members' relationships, the dimension that sustains the pair or group for the long term. It includes, for example, the way group members respect and care for one another, their level of trust and openness, and their general effectiveness as a working pair or group. Cutting across

---

Box 1.3
Skills in Identifying Intervention Points

- Seeing both the task and relationship processes
- Noticing the progress of the group (the tasks at hand) and what helping and blocking interactions (relationships) are affecting it
- Deciding what intervention will be helpful and how it can be presented effectively
- Taking part verbally and nonverbally so the task moves toward completion and/or interactions are made more constructive

---

at right angles, the woof—the task dimension—represents the substantive work in which people are engaged from moment to moment, from day to day, and that marks the group's progress as members clarify an issue, set goals, and carry out their action plan.

These two dimensions represent *levels of awareness* among the participants and set up a "double consciousness" for group members. Generally, the more members can hold in mind both levels of awareness, the fuller will be their experience, the more mindful their behavior, and the more effective their process together. The skills of identifying intervention points (see Box 1.3) help us to watch both the warp (relationship interactions) and the woof (task discussion) and make a contribution that helps the group move forward.

Interventions might focus on the task ("We've mentioned a lot of ideas for action, now let's list them") or on relationships ("We seem to be frustrated with this issue and are beginning to attack each other. How about a 10-minute break to think about it?"). In both kinds of interventions, the crucial act is often to name the behavior you see and then to suggest an alternative or ask the others what might be done.

Using Straight Talk

Clean, clear, straightforward speaking from the mind and heart—that is straight talk (see Box 1.4). Although the prescription sounds simple, the skill is not easy to practice. Yet for clarity, trustworthiness, and efficiency in communications among busy educators, nothing else succeeds as well in helping develop your working relationships.

Consider first what it is *not*. Straight talk is not being rude or brutal, it is never intended to embarrass another, and it does not "dump on" or complain about others. On the other hand, as the term implies, straight talk does not sugar-coat or otherwise obscure the communication.

By speaking for yourself, using "I" to clarify your ownership of thoughts and feelings, you demonstrate some of the central attributes of straight talk: spelling out your assumptions and reasoning, taking personal responsibility, and offering others a clear view of who you are. Interestingly, straight talk tends to empower others because the directness is contagious.

Giving Feedback

One of William Blake's *Songs of Experience,* "A Poison Tree," begins with a stark contrast between the effects of expressing anger appropriately and of withholding or burying it:

> I was angry with my friend:
>
> I told my wrath, my wrath did end.
>
> I was angry with my foe:
>
> I told it not, my wrath did grow.

(Blake, 1968, p. 114)

Box 1.4
Straight Talk

- Use language that expresses your real opinion and demonstrates communication between equals.
  "I like . . ."; "I dislike . . .";
  "I disagree, but let's consider the options."
- Use statements, not questions masquerading as statements.
  "I'm ready to move on," not "Do you think we've talked about this enough?"
- Make assertions without unnecessary tentatives and qualifiers.
  "I want to take a break," not "Maybe we could take a break?"
- Talk *to,* not *about,* another person.
  "I like that idea, Gwen," not "That was a good idea she had."
- Make assertions without diminishing yourself or your point.
  "I think the best course is . . . ," not "You may not agree with this, but. . . ."
- As appropriate, include your reasons and feelings along with the "facts."
  "I'm really disappointed the workshops were cancelled. It's going to put off our math curriculum, and I was all geared up for the change."
- Speak for yourself; use the pronoun *I.*
  "I'm afraid of conflict," not "You're afraid" or "We're afraid."

SOURCE: Adapted from Jamison (1988).

Ironically, surfacing the anger with his friend enables the poet to let it die away, but concealing it actually feeds and enlarges his anger. In the poem, Blake imagines the unexpressed wrath as a poisonous tree, growing to produce an apple that finally kills his enemy: "In the morning glad I see / My foe outstretch'd beneath the tree" (p. 115).

We picture effective feedback in the center of a spectrum between two ineffective extremes: At one end is "burying it" or sharing no honest reactions with others; at the other is "sounding off," blurting your opinions and feelings about events and people at every turn. Each extreme has some appeal: We may be tempted not to speak out about objectionable behavior in another person, for example, to avoid conflict or retaliation; or we may be tempted to lash out in a vain attempt to force another to change. Because both alternatives typically have negative consequences, we consider giving effective feedback a central influencing skill.

An effective feedback message consists of verbally placing a person's behavior in front of him or her to let the person see what you see—through *your* eyes, so to speak. Feedback typically includes two main parts and looks like this:

- "When you . . . [describe the person's specific behavior], the effect is . . . [describe the specific effects on you or others]."
- "I want/believe/value . . . [state your desires or values clearly], and I'd prefer . . . [if the other person does not offer something, state what you want]."

Here is how a feedback message might sound. Imagine that Mary, chair of the staff development committee, is frustrated with Joe, who has not followed through on an offer he made. Mary might say, "Joe, you didn't notify the committee about our meeting, and it's going to be at least another week before we can meet again. I worry about the lost time, but even more important, I begin to wonder about your commitment to the project. When you're responsible for something, I really depend on you to carry it out."

Giving feedback effectively is a complex skill. It depends on a combination of timeliness and the attitude of both people. Through feedback, we share our insight and judgment with one another and enrich our collective understanding of what we are doing and how we are working—or not working—together. As you embark on building more collaborative relationships with your colleagues, you may find it among the most useful of the influencing skills.

With this initial description of the bedrock skills, we invite you to consider with us how these and related skills help to develop and sustain working relationships that produce collaboration in schools. As you read on, keep in mind the importance of attending to the relationship among you as well as to the tasks that bring you together to help your students and your school.

Resources

Three widely available guides to communication skills are *Handbook of Interpersonal Communication* by Knapp and Miller (1994); Robert Bolton's *People Skills: How to Assert Yourself, Listen to Others, and Resolve Conflicts* (1986); and John Robert Stewart's *Bridges Not Walls: A Book About Interpersonal Communication* (1982). For a book with particular application to schools, see Friend and Cook's *Interactions: Collaboration Skills for School Professionals* (1992). A training manual by Hedlund and Freedman, *Helping Through Listening and Influencing* (1981), has informed our discussion of listening skills.

For a brief introduction to giving feedback, see Porter's "Giving Effective Feedback" (1995). A helpful and enjoyable book on feedback skills is *What Did You Say? The Art of Giving and Receiving Feedback,* by Seashore, Seashore, and Weinberg (1991). Two short, readable descriptions of "straight talk" can be found in Wasley's "Straight Shooting" (1995) and Jamison's "Straight Talk: A Norm-Changing Intervention" (1988).

For concise descriptions of interpersonal skills and group process and for techniques we have found useful with groups, we return often to *The Fifth Discipline Fieldbook: Strategies and Tools for Building a Learning Organization,* by Senge, Kleiner, Roberts, Ross, and Smith (1994).

A classic treatment of group theory and practice is *Joining Together: Group Theory and Group Skills* by Johnson and Johnson (1994). We also find useful Dimock's *Groups: Leadership and Group Development* (1987) and Bertcher's *Group Participation* (1994). We include additional resources about working in groups at the end of Chapters 4 through 8.

References

Bertcher, H. (1994). *Group participation*. Thousand Oaks, CA: Sage.
Blake, W. (1968). *The portable Blake* (A. Kazin, Ed.). New York: Viking.

Bolton, R. (1986). *People skills: How to assert yourself, listen to others, and resolve conflicts.* New York: Simon & Schuster.

Dimock, H. G. (1987). *Groups: Leadership and group development.* San Diego: University Associates.

Franklin, B. (1945). The spirit of compromise: An appeal for acceptance of the Constitution notwithstanding defects. In N. G. Goodman (Ed.), *A Benjamin Franklin reader* (pp. 353-355). New York: Thomas Y. Crowell.

Friend, M., & Cook, L. (1992). *Interactions: Collaboration skills for school professionals.* New York: Longman.

Hedlund, D. E., & Freedman, L. B. (1981). *Helping through listening and influencing.* Ithaca, NY: Cornell University, Department of Education.

Jamison, K. (1988, July). Straight talk: A norm-changing intervention. *National Training Laboratories Connections Newsletter, 5,* 1-2.

Johnson, D. W., & Johnson, F. P. (1994). *Joining together: Group theory and group skills* (5th ed.). Englewood Cliffs, NJ: Prentice Hall.

Knapp, M. L., & Miller, G. R. (1994). *Handbook of interpersonal communication.* Thousand Oaks, CA: Sage.

Latzko, W. (1995). *Four days with Dr. Deming: A strategy for modern methods of communication.* Reading, MA: Addison-Wesley.

Lawler, E. (1986). *High-involvement management.* San Francisco: Jossey-Bass.

Porter, L. C. (1995). Giving effective feedback: If we don't know it's broken, how can we fix it? In R. A. Ritvo, A. H. Litwin, & L. Butler (Eds.), *Managing in the age of change* (pp. 89-97). New York: Irwin.

Seashore, C. N., Seashore, E. W., & Weinberg, G. M. (1991). *What did you say? The art of giving and receiving feedback.* North Attleborough, MA: Douglas Charles.

Senge, P. (1990). *The fifth discipline: The art and practice of the learning organization.* New York: Doubleday.

Stewart, J. R. (1982). *Bridges not walls: A book about interpersonal communication.* Reading, MA: Addison-Wesley.

Wasley, P. (1995). Straight shooting. *Educational Leadership, 42*(8), 56-59.

Weisbord, M. (1987). *Productive workplaces: Organizing and managing for dignity, meaning, and community.* San Francisco: Jossey-Bass.

Wheatley, M. (1992). *Leadership and the new science.* San Francisco: Berrett-Koehler.

PART I

Pairs: The Power of Two

In the next two chapters, we invite you to consider two forms of collaboration widely practiced every day in schools: the consultative pair, in which one person asks another for help on a problem, and the paired team, in which two people work together around a shared purpose. Both kinds of pairs are eminently useful for a variety of needs at school, and although they require some "facilitating conditions" identified at the end of each chapter, they can flourish with relatively few special resources. Above all, both kinds of working pairs can reduce isolation, build collegial relationships, and make school work more creative and more satisfying.

Working pairs are probably the simplest forms of collaboration. A teacher, for example, unsure how to handle a difficult parent and confused after long sessions of solitary worry, drops in on a colleague and in a few minutes discovers an approach to the situation that seems just right. Or, to use our own case as joint authors of this book, we discovered a mutual interest in collaboration, schools, and writing— and different skills and experiences that seemed to us to complement each other—and decided to write this book together.

But the apparent simplicity of pairing up can be deceptive. Often it *looks* like a simple step from solitary work to work in a pair, but it is almost always a large leap. Perhaps the first law of collaborating in pairs is that working with another person is far more complex than working alone. The corollary is that the results two people produce are always different from (and probably better than) the results one of them would have produced alone. In short, although pairing up has a way of looking easy, it can be challenging, especially at the outset as both partners develop a common approach not only to the tasks they take on but also to their own working relationship.

Our experience both as consultants to others and as members of many pairs ourselves points to two attitudes that help to ensure a successful working pair: (a) a careful, deliberate approach to the various tasks involved in building the relationship and (b) a spirit of mutual discovery and learning about each other and the joint work. Like all other attitudes, these depend heavily on a well-developed set of skills. Essential to a deliberate approach to working in a pair and a spirit of joint learning are the bedrock skills described in Chapter 1, particularly listening skills that draw the other person out and clarify what both persons want and where they stand. Moreover, the four-phase process of convening, contracting, composing, and following through offers a way to build the relationship carefully, deliberately, in the context of the pair's evolving work.

The two attitudes interweave and reinforce each other. Respecting and caring for your colleague brings openness and a heightened sense of learning and mutual discovery. By learning together, clarifying your purposes, and negotiating your differences, you solidify the relationship and create a strong foundation for your work together. That is the promise of working pairs, and the power of two generates a kind of satisfaction and creativity that you, as one, cannot.

With this brief background, consider with us the consultative pair in Chapter 2 and the team of two in Chapter 3.

2

Giving and Receiving Help

The Consultative Pair

The last child had finally collected his pencils and books and left for the day. Peter was trying to tidy up after the day's hurricane of children when Helen, the teacher next door, wandered in. He could tell she was down. And it wasn't the first time. Increasingly in the past weeks, Helen had dropped by like this to seek Peter's counsel. Helen was in her second year at Tingley Middle School. Peter was in his seventeenth.

"Oh, Peter, I don't think I'm going to make it," Helen opened. "I've got 2 weeks till the grading period ends, and I haven't a clue what to do with Stanley. Here it is January. I've tried everything I can think of, and he's still climbing the walls after 15 minutes of class. I just don't know what I'm going to say to his parents this time."

"Believe me, Helen, we've all had our Stanleys—and plenty of them. I know how you feel."

"Those new reading materials were terrific for him," Helen went on, "and so was the new reading group I had him in. But it lasted just about 8 days!"

"Come on, let's go down to the teachers' room and grab a few minutes together over coffee. Maybe we can come up with a new option or two," Peter said, collecting his last few papers.

* * * *

Later that afternoon in the Tingley School office, Maggie Coughlin had just sat down for what felt like the first time all day. It had been another typical day for Maggie as principal, one full of brushfires and unexpected events. She had no sooner begun to relax when Nat Douglas burst into the room, his huge frame shaking with frustration.

"That's it!" he hollered, "I've had it. If that team won't work, I'm quitting as coach! They're nothing but a bunch of animals—no respect, no discipline, no nothin'!"

"Hold on, Nat!" Maggie cut in, "Don't you go doing anything rash, now. Just sit down a minute and tell me about it."

Nat was halfway to her visitor's chair when he blurted, "You know what this team has been like, Maggie. I don't need to tell you. I've never seen such a group of prima donnas in my life, and I can't make them play like a team! I don't know what it is about kids today, but I'm ready to hang it up with this business!"

Incidents like these two are played out every day in schools. Helen and Nat have reached the end of their rope with Stanley and the basketball team. They have been playing out that rope for some time, trying different strategies, hoping that one will turn Stanley or the team around. Today, they have come to Peter and Maggie for help—an attentive ear, a solution, partnership, permission to try something new, encouragement.

These two incidents are examples of a frequent occurrence among educators; one person comes to another for help with a difficult problem in his or her own practice. We say this is a frequent occurrence advisedly. In our experience, educators consult with each other when they can; the truth is that many conditions conspire against their doing it as often as they all may wish or need to. Pride, lack of time, the seeming inaccessibility of willing colleagues, and the sheer complexity and stress of daily work often make seeking help very difficult indeed.

In this chapter, we explore this type of help-centered interaction among educators. Several attributes of these interactions are noteworthy. First, one person *feels the need for some kind of assistance*; Helen and Nat come to Peter and Maggie because they cannot resolve a challenge alone. Second, they come to Peter and Maggie *because they see them as a resource:* in Peter's case, because he is the veteran teacher next door and presumably someone who has faced and resolved problems with other "Stanleys" in years past; in Maggie's case, because she is the principal and presumably has the authority and expertise to help Nat out with his team—or out of coaching altogether. Next, Helen and Nat bring their problems to Peter and Maggie *under pressure, with a sense of urgency.* They are unable to resolve their problems alone, and the problems have not gone away, so they have appeared in Peter's room and Maggie's office with "something important riding on this." Finally, as is all too common in school problem solving, *time is short:* Helen feels the impending crisis that will come at the end of the grading period when Stanley fails again; Nat needs a solution *tonight* so that he can pull his team together tomorrow and presumably for the next game. On top of these deadlines, neither pair of educators has a lot of time (or energy) today to solve these persisting problems.

Certainly, all occasions of seeking help do not have this urgency or the levels of frustration that Helen and Nat are feeling. In many schools, educators quite calmly exchange questions, answers, suggestions, and ideas as a matter of course. We suggest that you and your colleagues can make such consultations a more naturally occurring process by using a framework that supports a helping relationship between two people.

With the four-phase framework outlined in Chapter 1—convening, contracting, composing, and following through—you face critical choices in each phase of a consultative relationship with a colleague. How each of you resolves the questions in each phase helps to define the relationship and determine its effectiveness. Let us consider the central tasks that arise in the course of the consultative relationship.

Convening

The person seeking help usually begins the convening phase by selecting someone who seems able to provide just the right kind of help. As you find yourself in that situation, it is useful at the outset to ask yourself, "What kind of help do I need?" and to consider the suggestions listed in Box 2.1.

Nat, for example, needs solid emotional support and may need the power of the school's authority to deal with the team's behavior.

**Box 2.1
What Kind of Help Do I Need?**

In any given situation, consider where on the following spectrum your own needs fall:

- Simple listening (just to be heard)
- Emotional support
- Analytical support (to understand the problem)
- Technical support (to expand your resources)
- Advice and guidance
- Help in carrying out your tasks

Knowing those needs helps him to select Maggie the principal as his helper and to begin their consultative relationship with clarity and directness.

Next, ask, "What am I looking for in a helper?" If you simply need a sounding board, for example, you may select a person who is both peer and friend and who will listen without judging or advising. If you need advice and guidance, then you are likely to consider people with longer or more varied experience than you have, who also have a track record of being attentive, trustworthy, and sympathetic. Regardless of the specific need, above all other qualities a helper can possess, these two stand out: the ability to concentrate on you and to listen without judging.

A final question arises in the area of clarifying needs: "When should I seek help?" If you have a clear need and know the kind of help you want and who your potential helpers are, our advice is simple: Don't wait! Find the help as early as possible, before additional complications set in.

Contracting

This phase of the consultative relationship is crucial to its success because it ensures that *both* of you willingly join in a partnership and understand your parts in it. Contracting need not be formal, but it must bring clarity about the purposes and roles of you both. Let us look at each aspect in turn.

Negotiating Your Joint Purpose

As we have seen, the person seeking help typically begins by reaching out to you, the potential helper, talking about the problem, trying to be clear about the kind of help needed, and perhaps also testing your helping skills—a number of not-so-easy tasks (Box 2.2 lists some questions he or she may want to consider). For you as helper, on the other hand, being approached in this way also brings up several crucial questions.

First, "Am I available now?" The moment Helen entered Peter's room and Nat stormed into Maggie's office, Peter and Maggie faced a choice: Will I and can I hear this person's

---

Box 2.2
Seeking Help: Questions to Consider

You can work toward greater clarity about the problem and also about the helper by asking yourself questions such as

- Is the helper attentive?
- Does he or she take you and your issue seriously enough?
- Is the issue getting clearer as you and the helper talk?
- Does the helper stray into "solving your problem" or giving long-winded responses?
- Are you as comfortable in this conversation as you hoped to be?

---

problem right now? Although this might seem an insignificant question, it is very important to the future of the working relationship between the individuals in these pairs. Peter and Maggie are not likely to be of assistance if they are not ready to be fully present and to listen to Helen or Nat's issues and feelings. If the weight of their own day is so great that they do not have the time or the energy to devote to Helen or Nat at that moment, they may take some time to get ready to help (much as Peter suggests a walk to the coffee machine) or else suggest another time altogether.

Second, "Is the other person being specific about the kind of help he or she wants?" If not, it is useful to ask because the question can help clarify what may become the joint purpose. Be patient at this point, because the other person may not fully know what help is needed, especially if he or she is feeling stress. To reach clarity, use interviewing and questioning skills to draw the other person out (see Chapter 1 and the "Composing" section below).

Third, "Am I able to help in this way?" This question poses real choices for you about both your capacity and your desire to help. For good reasons, you may decide not to take on the helping role. You may be in the throes of dealing with a problem of your own, for instance, and may not be able to offer the attention the other person needs. Choosing to be a helper makes most sense when you can be fully present and when you feel fairly comfortable with the kind of problem presented and the level of your bedrock skills (especially listening skills). If you have any hesitations about helping, discussing them now serves to clarify whether you should proceed and, if so, your shared sense of purpose in the consultation. Ideally, negotiating the purpose is a mutual exploration toward a shared decision about continuing the consultation.

Negotiating Your Individual Roles

In contracting, you each make choices that define your roles and relationship around this problem and strongly influence how you behave in this consultation. Too often ignored, this negotiation is highly useful. Talking about your respective roles can help to clarify expectations and set ground rules for this relationship. You also practice "straight talk" with one another from the beginning (see Chapter 1).

As the person seeking help, you might consider these aspects of a desirable role for yourself:

- Keeping control of the agenda, including the boundaries of the discussion (e.g., what to include, when to end)
- Being free to express all your thoughts and feelings in safety and confidentiality
- Being thorough about the problem and considering all options that arise
- Being authentic with the helper, providing suggestions and feedback about how both of you are working together

As the helper, on the other hand, your essential choice is to determine how much ownership over the problem you will take. When Helen and Nat come to Peter and Maggie, the problems they bring are theirs alone. Peter and Maggie decide to *consult* with Helen and Nat, helping them come to their own solution and follow-through, rather than *joining* with them in the solution and follow-through (we explore the latter option in the next chapter). In our experience, the most effective help usually follows from the helper's commitment to care about the partner's problem but not to take it on him- or herself (see Box 2.3 for key elements of the helper's role). This stance allows you to sustain the role of helper and to provide perspective from outside the problem itself.

When you both are clear about your purpose and different roles in the consultation, you can move into the composing phase, confident in the relationship you have established with each other.

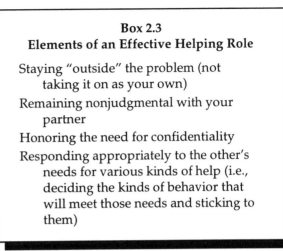

Box 2.3
Elements of an Effective Helping Role

Staying "outside" the problem (not taking it on as your own)

Remaining nonjudgmental with your partner

Honoring the need for confidentiality

Responding appropriately to the other's needs for various kinds of help (i.e., deciding the kinds of behavior that will meet those needs and sticking to them)

Composing

As the person seeking help, your task is first to clarify the problem; then to identify and explore your options, coming to a commitment to action; and finally, to take action and review it with your helper. This description sounds too simple and too rational, of course. We imagine that for Helen and Nat, the work of articulating their problems, examining their meaning, and exploring options is relatively complex and difficult. What can help to ease the burden is your own ability to bring up all the relevant issues and the helper's bedrock skills.

As the helper, on the other hand, your main job is to draw out your partner. As we suggested in Chapter 1, the bedrock skills begin with being fully present—demonstrating that you are willing to "be with" your partner by simply paying attention. Imagine how Maggie's arrangement of the physical space in her office would signal different things to Nat. A huge desk, piled with documents, might suggest aloofness: "I'm too busy for you." One of us worked with a school principal who, to show he was ready to listen, would collect all the papers and files open on his desk, stack them to the side, and look out, smiling, over a completely clear space. That kind of presence, that level of attention, affirms that you value your partner and encourages his or her trust in you.

Up to this point, Helen and Nat have not understood the problem sufficiently to see ways to deal with it effectively. So the substance of the helping involves clarifying what the problem is, striving for new understandings of it, and designing strategies for acting differently with Stanley and the team tomorrow. Several of the bedrock skills are especially useful.

Interviewing

Your questions, appropriately framed and timed, help both of you in several ways:

- They guide your partner to explore thoughts, feelings, opinions, and memories.
- They draw out your partner and thus help to accomplish the initial work of the consultation.
- They help you to resist the urge to assume, advise, offer opinions, and judge.
- They clarify, for both of you, the meaning you are creating together.

Bear in mind, as we suggested in Chapter 1, that open questions are particularly useful. Closed questions—those that often can be answered with a single word or phrase—may work well in the courtroom, where guardedness and hostility prevail, but they have limited use in a consultation. Open questions work to expand awareness, as in these questions that Peter and Maggie might ask their partners:

- "Would you tell me more about Stanley's behavior?"
- "Tell me what you see happening among the team members."
- "What happened for you when the team fell apart out on the field?"

When you ask for more information, your partner's response makes the information available to both of you; the issue becomes clear—even to the speaker—as it is put into words. That is the real service the helper performs, through questions and also through another essential listening skill: reflecting.

Reflecting

As we suggested in Chapter 1, in a reflection you gather the essence of what your partner has been saying—thoughts, feelings, facts—and then offer it back in compressed form for his or her review. Let us take an example from Peter's conversation with Helen. Helen describes her problem by saying, "I don't think I'm going to make it. I've got 2 weeks till the grading period ends, and I haven't a clue what to do with Stanley. . . . I just don't know what I'm going to say to his parents this time."

Peter, after inviting Helen to join him for coffee in the teacher's room and asking a few more questions, might make a reflection like this: "I can tell you're really frustrated that Stanley hasn't responded so far, and you're wondering if there are any options that *will* work, especially in such a short time. You're also concerned about how his parents will respond when you tell them about his lack of progress. Is that right?"

Sometimes a reflection creates immediate insight in your partner, even leading directly to a sense of how to resolve the problem. Often solutions are implicit in the problem, and what the partner needs most is assistance clarifying just what the problem is. Most important, your task in reflections is to place in front of your partner the thoughts and feelings you have heard, with the faith that he or she will ultimately respond to such clarity with a realization of what can be done. The person needing help, not the helper, holds the key.

Summarizing

If good reflections make good helpers, so do good summaries (see Chapter 1), especially when you make them at strategic points in your consultations: after a complex exchange, toward the end of a session, and at the beginning of a subsequent conversation. Summaries help to focus attention and prepare for further work. Unlike a reflection, your own contributions to the conversation can be included in a summary, and also you can ask your partner if he or should would like to summarize where things stand; this technique is especially useful after you have explored the options together but before your partner has made a decision.

Giving Feedback

In helping relationships, there may be an occasional need to offer your partner feedback. Box 2.4 suggests some conditions for effective feedback.

Box 2.4
Giving Feedback

Giving feedback can be immensely
helpful to your partner, but it
requires several conditions for
success:

- It must be offered to be helpful,
  not to hurt.
- It focuses on specific behavior or
  statements.
- It is offered skillfully, gently (and
  infrequently!).
- It is best when offered in the spirit
  of sharing information, not giving
  advice.

It is a primary way for you, as helper, to move beyond a strictly receptive or "supportive" role and place before your partner something of which he or she is not yet aware—some inconsistency between his statements and behavior, for instance, or a pattern of behavior that, though invisible to your partner, may contribute to the problem he or she faces.

Let us say, for instance, that Helen, talking with Peter in the teachers' room, has continued to express reluctance about seeing Stanley's parents again because she finds Stanley's behavior beyond her control. Peter might offer Helen feedback in this way: "Helen, you've said several times that facing Stanley's parents is going to be hard for you, and you've also said that you can't think of more ways to settle him down. It looks as if you're feeling completely responsible for Stanley—like you're thinking maybe his behavior comes from some failure on your part. I wonder if that rings true." Helen might pause, then respond with "Good lord, Peter, you're right! I've been assuming that if I just knew more, I'd have Stanley shaped up in no time. But this isn't my fault at all!"

Or, of course, Helen might say, "No, that's not it at all." That response demonstrates that there is risk in giving feedback—the risk of being wrong. Yet if the relationship is grounded in trust and your feedback, even if inaccurate, comes out of your desire to help, there is no harm done. The essential aspects of your helping role are still intact, and you can continue the conversation.

Giving Advice

Before concluding this discussion of the helper's work, we must add a word about another influencing skill: giving advice. We noted above that in its most nondirective form, helping another person excludes offering advice and relies on faith in the partner's ability to solve his or her own problems. However, giving advice *when it is requested* does not necessarily violate that faith. Deciding when and how to offer advice depends to a great extent on the strength of the relationship between you and your colleague.

Here are some considerations when you are tempted to give or are asked for your opinion about a person or situation:

- If you state it, your opinion about a person or group that your partner feels strongly about will alter the course of the consultation in one way or another. If your opinions coincide, the level of trust between you may rise, but your partner may resist seeing another point of view. If your opinions differ, stating your opinion may help by bringing a fresh viewpoint, but your partner may focus on disagreement and choose to argue the point. In general, offering this kind of opinion is risky and promises little benefit.
- If your partner asks you for advice about what to do, you might suggest that you both focus on the problem first, or that you both brainstorm options together. If he or she asks for advice after exploring the options, you could ask (gently) why your preference is important right now. Ultimately, if you offer your opinion, give it as your own preference about what *you* would do in this situation, and add your reasons.

The sustaining principle here is the importance of honoring the contract you have established. As helper and help seeker, you share a mission, but your roles are quite different, as is your work in the consultation.

Following Through

As in many relationships, this crucial step can easily be lost in the shuffle by busy educators. It must not be lost. If you are the one seeking help, you have developed by this point a new idea or course of action with your colleague, but now you are left to try it out in the same old situations where new strategies have probably failed before. On top of that, you are probably left to try them alone. To offset these conditions, we urge you to continue your relationship with your helper. Tell your colleague what you intend to do, and ask him or her to meet with you again so you both can review the situation as it evolves.

In the same way, as the helper, encourage your partner; offer to help him or her rehearse new strategies beforehand and assess new developments as following through proceeds. By such continuing attention, you say in effect, "I cannot do this for you, but I sure want you to succeed." By being there at the end of the day, the basketball practice, or even the next morning to ask, "Oh, how did it go?" you say, "I care about you and about your success with kids." This is the stuff of long-standing working relationships.

Finally, we encourage both partners in the consultation, when it is over, to close it up. Informal consultative relationships (as opposed, for example, to mentoring relationships) can become counterproductive if stretched out too far beyond the original problem. Despite the best intentions, the helper's role can mutate into a narrow parentalism, and the help seeker can become dependent (and then counterdependent, of course) rather than empowered to act. The relationship between the two people can continue to flourish if they both agree on an explicit ending to the consultation. It is a good time for thanks, reflecting back on your work together, and reaffirming the value of your relationship as colleagues.

Facilitating Conditions

As we noted in the Introduction, we close Chapters 2 through 8 by noting some specific conditions that facilitate the form of collaboration each chapter explores. In Chapter 9, we revisit these conditions and suggest approaches for nurturing them in schools.

Given the importance of consultative pairs as a way to embody a collegial norm and encourage widespread collaboration, what conditions at school support and foster their work? Consider these:

- A private place to talk together (not the hallway!)
- Time for the pair to connect and talk; some schools devote weekly after-school time to refreshments and idea exchanges when teachers can find partners with helpful ideas
- The opportunity, especially for the help seeker, to reflect, plan, and prepare for new action

- A culture and norms that support both asking for help and giving help (modeled, for instance, by school leaders)
- A climate of experimentation—one that supports inquiry into practice and risk taking with new teaching and student management practices

Resources

The Resources section in Chapter 1 contains books and articles on the bedrock skills. Beyond those, here are several works relevant for the consultative pair. For a venerable treatment of communication skills in school, focusing on teachers and students, see Gordon's *Teacher Effectiveness Training* (1993). Friend and Cook's *Interactions: Collaboration Skills for School Professionals* (1992) is a practical guide to interpersonal communication, problem solving, and consultation (see especially Chapters 2-4).

Little's work describing teacher-teacher collegial norms that support innovative practice can be found in her essay "Teachers as Colleagues" (1987).

Two classics by the psychologist Carl Rogers explore the principles and practice of the helping consultation: *Client Centered Therapy: Its Current Practices, Implications, and Theory* (1951) and *On Becoming a Person* (1961). The first develops Rogers' entire approach to nondirective counseling; the other builds from the first, with especially useful chapters on the helping role.

For further guidance about being an effective nonprofessional helper, see Kennedy's *On Becoming a Counselor: A Basic Guide for Non-Professional Counselors* (1977).

References

Friend, M., & Cook, L. (1992). *Interactions: Collaboration skills for school professionals.* New York: Longman.

Gordon, T. (1993). *Teacher effectiveness training.* New York: Random House. (Original work published 1975)

Kennedy, E. (1977). *On becoming a counselor: A basic guide for non-professional counselors.* New York: Seabury.

Little, J. W. (1987). Teachers as colleagues. In V. Richardson-Koehler (Ed.), *Educator's handbook: A research perspective* (pp. 491-518). New York: Longman.

Rogers, C. (1951). *Client centered therapy: Its current practices, implications, and theory.* Boston: Houghton Mifflin.

Rogers, C. (1961). *On becoming a person.* Boston: Houghton Mifflin.

3

Pairing Up

The Team of Two

It was 7:15 a.m. Sarah had just picked up Pam, and the two were settling in for their 20-minute drive to the Forest Avenue Elementary School. The two friends, both seasoned fourth-grade teachers, started talking immediately.

"Did you read that memo from the Super's office?" Sarah queried.

"Yes, yes! I looked at it last night," Pam answered excitedly. "I'm really tempted to apply for those funds. I mean, I've been thinking about hands-on science for ages, but I've never really been able to develop some units for it."

Sarah came in as if on cue: "Exactly what I was thinking! The innovative grant could give me the chance to do a bang-up job with my plant life unit."

"You know, Sarah, maybe we should do this together. We're right next door to each other. We've been working on the fourth-grade team for what, 10 years? This could be a great opportunity to do something about our science curriculum. What do you think?"

* * * *

11:15 a.m. Mark Castanza, a parent, continued to pace around Meg Thomas's office. Meg, a counselor at Forest Avenue, had been listening intently to Mark's concern.

"I'm really at my wits' end, Ms. Thomas," Mark was saying. "Danny seems to get along with a couple of his teachers, but he doesn't seem to know what Mr. Lanowski is talking about. He frets about English all the time. And he's not too sure about social studies either—Ms. Tenney's the teacher, and she . . . well, Danny just can't seem to catch the drift of what's happening in that class."

"I'm really glad you came in right away, Mark," Meg answered, then went on, "Oh, and by the way, please call me Meg. . . . Part of my job is to work with parents on problems their children are having. It can be hard for sixth graders at first, moving from one teacher to another, and that may be Danny's problem. I expect we can find a way to help him."

"It's so difficult being a single parent, trying to keep track of two kids and hold down a job. Danny's just getting to that age where he isn't listening to me the way he used to. So what is the story about these teachers? From what Danny says, the math and science teachers, like, work their lessons together. But Lanowski and the history teacher don't make it as clear. Looks to me like they've got different ways of going about things, and Danny's not catching on."

"Well, that sounds right to me, Mark," Meg responded. "The question is, how's Danny responding to these four different teachers. Maybe they'd have some insights about that."

"Yeah, I was thinking . . . what about talking with the teachers? We could sit down with them and talk about what seems to be happening. Maybe there's something I could be doing at home, helping with the assignments or something. . . . What d'you think, could we talk to them together?" Mark asked.

These two short scenarios from Forest Avenue Elementary School introduce another type of working relationship commonly found in schools: the paired team. Unlike the relationship in Chapter 2, in which one person comes to another for assistance with his or her problem, these pairs *share* the problem or opportunity from the outset. They have a degree of mutuality that consulting pairs do not; both people have a commitment to a common goal because they believe it will contribute to their mission with children—as teachers, counselors, parents. These mutual pairings are potent ways to take action in schools. They are easy to convene and, with careful contracting and a strong relationship between partners, the phases of composing and following through can proceed without a vast investment of time and energy.

This type of working relationship is typified by three key attributes. First, as noted above, they emerge from a *mutual need, opportunity, or goal.* Sarah and Pam, for example, find during a casual conversation that they are independently weighing the possibility of writing a grant proposal for the same purpose. Second, *a good-faith relationship already exists;* the soil is prepared to support mutual planning and action. Sarah and Pam have developed a friendship and are next-door colleagues. Meg and Mark, although they have not had a personal relationship, have a professional relationship in which they are expected to work side by side to support Mark's child. Third, a degree of *mutuality characterizes the relationship* in that both partners accept responsibility for the need, problem, or opportunity they face. Although this is obvious in Pam's and Sarah's case, Mark and Meg also seem to accept a common responsibility. Mark has not come to Meg to blame Mr. Lanowski and the school for Danny's troubles, and he readily suggests that he and Meg team up.

Our four-phase framework is useful in building and sustaining these paired teams. In each phase, we identify a couple of important processes you can think about and use in your practice.

Convening

Paired teams often begin spontaneously. As we noted above, they often spring up where a relationship exists that either encourages this spontaneity or legitimizes two people coming together around a need, goal, or opportunity. In our scenarios above, both pairs experienced a moment when each person might have thought, "We could do this together." This sense of joint discovery is the hallmark of the convening phase.

Most paired teams have such a "convening moment," even though it might be recognizable only after the fact. One aspect—exploring the possibility of working in tandem—is a conscious choice, however. It states out loud both the goal and the desire to work together to reach it. Often the explicit suggestion comes after a lot of discussion. In our own case, for example, we had several long conversations about schools and teamwork before we talked about writing a book together. Sometimes, as in the short scenarios above, one person will drop the suggestion of tandem work into the discussion at the outset.

Whether this explicit proposal to team up comes early or late in the convening process, it revolves around two essential questions about the relationship between partners: "What am I looking for in a partner?" and "What are you looking for?" When one person suggests, as Pam did, that "maybe we should do this together," she is stating that the other person meets some basic criteria she has for a working partner. We suggest that you clarify for yourself what these criteria are. At the contracting phase of the process, it will help to share your expectations and perceptions about one another and the partnership as you build a strong working pair.

As you weigh the possibility of pairing up, consider the kinds of questions noted in Box 3.1. These are questions that future partners need to address alone.

We have found that answers to them are seldom certain; instead, each person has to feel that there is at least a fair chance for an affirmative answer in each case. Again thinking back to our own convening phase as joint authors, we both recall the growing sense that "this could really work out." That was enough for each of us to be able to say, "Sure, let's talk about what a book might look like."

Box 3.1
Guidelines for Thinking About Effective Working Partners

Do I respect and enjoy this person? Can I be honest with him or her, and do I think he or she can be with me?

Do my talents and skills complement his or hers?

Do I have the time, energy, and drive to commit to an equal partnership around this goal?

Would pairing up with him or her benefit my work as an educator or parent?

Contracting

When two equal partners discuss their mutual purpose and roles, their talk often has an evolving and indefinite quality. Pam might say to Sarah, "Yeah, now, how would this work? What type of hands-on science do you want to work on? And should we be developing the same units?" Exploring in this way is helpful at this point, but a week down the road, as they are outlining the innovative grant proposal, they will need to be a lot more specific about their goals and objectives, and their individual roles in their paired team will need greater definition. With each unexpected challenge or new turn of events, Sarah and Pam will need to remain ready to reevaluate their purpose and roles in relation to what is happening. In a sense, their contracting will continue throughout their work on this project.

The initial contracting process can illustrate the essential aspects of this ongoing work. First, Meg and Mark and Pam and Sarah need to clarify their purpose to a level necessary for each partner to commit to it. Second, they need to discuss what each partner brings to the pair—in the eyes of each person. And third, they need to agree on some ground rules for how they will maintain their working relationship and accomplish their task. Let us look at each aspect in turn.

The pair need to clarify their mutual goal enough that each partner can feel and articulate a commitment to work together to attain it. The goal and the mutual commitment are like colored strands in a braid, weaving together, then moving apart and then weaving back together repeatedly over the course of the working relationship. This is the beauty of paired teams: They are flexible, they are easy to convene and maintain, and as long as each partner can participate honestly, the purpose and commitment levels can be renegotiated to meet the needs of each partner.

The guidelines suggested in Box 3.2 can help you to monitor your purpose and commitment as you become a paired team. Such direct questions require honest self-reflection; individually writing down your thoughts

---

Box 3.2
Initial Contracting Guidelines

- Open sharing by each person about his or her aspirations:

  "What do I hope to accomplish by this work?"

- Open declaration of the overlaps and gaps between the partners' individual goals and aspirations:

  "How are our goals alike? How are they different?"

- Open conversation about each person's commitment to a purpose statement reflecting overlapping goals:

  "What could we accomplish as a pair?" (It can help to write your answers in several simple goal statements, starting with "We hope to . . .")

  "Do I feel excited by this goal and by working with you to reach it?"

  "Given everything else I'm doing right now, will this excitement sustain me so I can do my share to make it work?"

before discussing them together can help. Then have a candid talk with your partner. This is not the time for superficial politeness! Contracting requires straight talk and grappling with real questions. We recommend that you listen carefully to yourself and monitor your feelings about this budding commitment.

The second contracting activity can be helpful in bringing up doubts and worries. We suggest that open dialogue about what each partner brings to the partnership can have impressive benefits. The essential qualities of this dialogue are two: It creates and affirms the basic equality of the two partners, and it teaches the pair about each partner's talents, style, and challenges. The dialogue informs each partner about the other so that together they can make informed choices about whether and how to proceed as a team. The roles that the partners take in the work together need to capitalize on their individual strengths and interests.

Discovering talents and skills that are relevant to the pair's goals can happen best once the pair has clarified the goals and some strategies for reaching them. We include suggestions for this process in the "Composing" section of this chapter. We also recommend, during the contracting phase, that each person ask him- or herself:

- What do I do well that I can bring to this pair?
- What do I see in my partner that reassures me?
- How do our styles of thinking, teaching, and working with others fit together?

Spending some time discussing the answers to these questions begins the important process of identifying what your strengths are as a paired team.

Finally, the contracting process always benefits from clarity about how the partners will work together. We recommend that you discuss and agree on ground rules for your working relationship—how to act with one another so this team will succeed. These need not be written, but they need to be discussed, and, most important, you each need to feel secure that you understand and accept the plan for working together. Peter Senge and his colleagues (see Box 3.3) suggest ground rules for "skillful discussion" that make a good starting point.

A pair's ground rules, it seems to us, need at a minimum to include the following:

- When, where, and how you as a pair will commit time and energy to the work you have defined for yourselves
- How you will ensure that feelings will be discussed insofar as they are affecting the work and the relationship
- Straight talk about the task (see Chapter 1)
- Straight talk about your performance: sharing feedback from other sources on your work, sharing feedback on one another's participation, and developing ways to strengthen individual participation and teamwork (see Chapter 1)
- Whom you might contact if you find yourselves in a conflict you cannot resolve and need the help of a skilled, neutral outsider (anticipating such a need now can make it easier for you to manage such a situation if it arises later on)

As we turn to the composing phase, we want to emphasize that in each step of the contracting process, both partners always have the option to say, "I don't think I can do this anymore." That choice needs to be affirmed repeatedly because the success of the pair in moving their idea into action will depend on the basic equality of their partnership. Pam will feel abandoned if she and Sarah write a successful grant, only to have Sarah later pull back from the curriculum planning and implementation. Similarly, if Meg and Mark do not understand and follow through on their individual responsibilities in organizing the sixth-grade teachers for Danny's benefit, they run a risk that one or both of them will later feel let down.

Box 3.3
Suggestions for "Skillful Discussion"

1. Pay attention to your intentions.
   What do I want right now? Am I willing to be influenced?
2. Balance influencing with listening.
   "What led you to that view?" "What do you mean by that view?"
3. Build shared understanding.
   "When we use the term _____, what do we really mean?"
4. Use self-awareness as a resource.
   What am I thinking? What am I feeling?
5. Explore impasses without judgment.
   "What do we agree on, and what do we disagree on?"

SOURCE: Adapted from P. Senge et al. (1994). The fifth discipline fieldbook (p. 390). New York: Doubleday Currency.

Composing

In pursuit of their joint mission, the two people in a paired team face two kinds of work: making progress on substantive tasks to reach their goal and maintaining an open, mutual working relationship. The first of these is often straightforward for the pair. Substantive work often takes the form of several steps in the planning process: setting realistic objectives, brainstorming strategies for reaching them, identifying actions to be taken, scheduling, and dividing responsibilities for follow-through.

One of the strengths of a paired team is its flexibility to devise its own planning and implementation steps and to adjust quickly to unforeseen events and opportunities. Depending on the situation, the pair might follow these steps informally and loosely. Mark and Meg agreed on their initial goal and strategy almost immediately (to learn more about Danny's teachers by going to meet them) and did so without using the jargon of planning. But Sarah and Pam are more likely to use the steps consciously, trying to be as complete as possible in their more formal task of curriculum development and proposal writing.

The second major aspect of a paired team's work is to sustain the quality of the relationship, both for itself and for the sake of the team's mission. If the pair have contracted carefully, they have already created a strong basis on which to build. They have worked out their goals, developed joint commitment, and established some ground rules to guide their working relationship.

Because mutuality is the hallmark of the paired team, each partner carries equal weight as the team creates a common meaning and plan, weaving the product by alternately giving and receiving, influencing and listening. The image of weaving is especially useful. The work of collaboration differs from solo work because it is accomplished, not first in one person's mind and then in the other's, but on the loom between them, in the center of their joint space.

The richness of paired collaboration, as well as its biggest challenges, lies in effectively acknowledging and, where appropriate, resolving the differences between the partners. The advantage of the paired team over individual work lies in deploying individual differences so that "the whole is greater than the sum of the parts." We have found four kinds of differences especially germane to the collaborative pair: differences of status, style, understanding, and talent.

Differences of Status

The issue here is how to sustain personal equality between the two of you. As an example, let us say that you are an assistant principal and that your partner on this project, Mike, is an English teacher. You have talked about this status difference while contracting and have agreed to work on an equal footing. Some ways in which you might deepen that sense of equality include meeting in Mike's room or a "neutral" spot—anywhere but your office. Consider beginning your conversation with a "check-in," a highly useful way to become fully present with yourself and your partner (see Chapter 1, under "Listening Skills"): Each of you takes a few minutes to tell the other what the day has involved for you, how you are feeling about the project, and simply what is happening for you right now. A check-in emphasizes our common humanity and encourages us to talk as equals.

Turn taking is helpful as well. Status differences often make one person defer to the other. Partners who remain alert to the balance of talk, work, and responsibility between them and who can discuss perceived imbalances can guard against feelings of inequality. Most important, if status raises itself as an issue at any point, straight talk will take you right back to the contracting phase, where you can explore and resolve the issue again.

Differences of Style

These are differences in operational styles—how the two partners like to work. Work style differences are bound to surface in pairs and groups and can be frustrating or worse if not acknowledged and dealt with.

An important principle about operational styles is that they represent our *preferences*; at some point, often early in our lives, we all developed certain styles that worked well or seemed more useful than others. When working closely with a partner, these styles will become more and more obvious as you take on and execute tasks. We can illustrate this point by drawing on the Myers-Briggs Type Indicator (MBTI), developed by Isabel Myers from the psychological typology of Carl Jung. The MBTI has popularized four contrasting styles: introversion and extraversion; sensing and intuition; thinking and feeling; and, one of the most fundamental stylistic differences affecting people at work, "perception" (P) and "judgment" (J). (If you would like to learn more about the MBTI, see Myers, 1980.)

In a paired team, a strong "P" may begin to wander around the task, captivated by some association that leads out into attractive but not fully relevant byways. Meanwhile, a "J" partner, seeing the partner wander off and unable to move toward a decision, may become increasingly anxious. Or, early in the discussion of possible strategies to pursue, the "J" partner may become impatient with what seems like an endless series of possibilities and may push for a decision just when it would benefit them both to explore the possibilities, mulling over them until some clarity develops.

Both preferences have strengths and weaknesses; the trick in a paired team with both styles represented is to capitalize on the strengths and minimize the weaknesses. Two implications are important here. First, for the most part our natural styles are neither right nor wrong, good nor bad—they are simply how we have chosen to operate. Second, they are not absolute in us—we can modify our style to accommodate our partner's.

Here are several suggestions to help you identify or address differences of style:

- Use agendas (formal or informal) when you meet.
    1. Develop an agenda together when you start your discussion (what can you accomplish in the time you have today?).
    2. Refer to the agenda when either one of you feels you have gone off task.
- Agree to confirm decisions with one another.
    1. Agree to brainstorm alternatives (for the rules of brainstorming, see Chapter 4).
    2. When one of you has reached a decision, test it out with the other.
    3. Agree that you both must feel comfortable with the decision and that if either of you is not, you will explore more options until you both find a more comfortable one.
- Bring up your feelings and needs; simply acknowledging these differences and affirming them is often all you will need to do.
    1. Agree that it is OK to talk about differences between you.
    2. Agree that when you are not sure how your partner is feeling about your work together or about you, you will ask him or her directly.

Implicit Assumptions

Finding a common language is always a challenge; thus one of the ground rules of "skillful discussion" is to agree on the meaning of key words. Beyond that, there is a related yet even more daunting problem: how implicit assumptions can control our thought, distort communication, and disrupt a pair's work. Suppose, for example, that Meg the counselor, as she watched Mark pace around her office, began to assume that Mark would simply vent his frustration at Danny's teachers if he had the opportunity. On that basis, she might well have decided that a meeting of Mark and the teachers would be premature, and she would have suggested another way to proceed. Thus the whole course of their problem solving might well have swerved off track, and their relationship as a paired team of equals would have had little chance to develop.

Two aspects of assumptions make them particularly insidious. First, they develop just below the level of consciousness and constitute what we take for granted as true about the world. We build them into our reality, our sense of what is normal. Second, the source of assumptions almost always has an *apparent* validity: If Mark expresses frustration with Meg, maybe he could blow up with the teachers!

Assumptions can surface in stereotypes or beliefs about other people and their differences from us. These affect how we work with one another in ways that are, at first, unknown to us. Assumptions about differences between men and women, teachers and administrators, and educators and parents, as well as about differences stemming from religious, ethnic, or racial identities, can influence our expectations of one another and our communications (see Locke, 1992; Tannen, 1990).

To help make assumptions explicit, we recommend two ways of asking questions (see Box 3.4). The first is internal, raising into awareness the assumptions that form in the twilight levels of our own minds. When you uncover the assumptions, you can decide whether or not to share them; often just by bringing them up into your own awareness, you strip them of much of their power.

The second way is spoken, asking questions that work to reveal your partner's assumptions. This helps your partner gain clarity, of course, but it also helps both of you to deepen your joint understanding and keep your "loom" clear of the debris of assumptions. The questions are simple techniques for gently inviting your partner

---

Box 3.4
Discovering Implicit Assumptions

Ask questions of yourself:

- "What am I assuming about this topic?"
- "What am I assuming about her behavior?"
- "What am I assuming about his motives?"

Ask questions of your partner:

- "What's behind your suggestion? I'd like to understand better where you're coming from."
- "Can you say more about what you think will happen?"
- "Any assumptions there?"

---

to find and open up important assumptions influencing your progress.

Differences of Talent

In our discussion of the contracting phase, we suggested that a pair explore differences of talent and how their various strengths and weaknesses might complement one another. The subject will usually come up again after partners have identified actions to take and as they are dividing responsibilities. Your effectiveness as a team will be enhanced if you can deploy your skills and talents to take advantage of each individual's strengths.

Here the two members' abilities can demonstrate immediately the usefulness of differences. Let us imagine that Pam and Sarah, working on their grant proposal, already know from their long friendship that Pam does not like to write; she can draw, however, and she puts together great presentations. Sarah agrees to write up the first draft of the proposal after the two have developed the content together. Pam will add several illustrations to the proposal and will take the lead on presenting it to the funding board if they make the cut. In such ways, paired teams can capitalize on their different skills.

As you identify collaborative actions to be taken, consider the various contacts and connections each of you has. In the case of Meg and Mark, for example, it would be natural for her to initiate contact with Danny's teachers, preparing for the meetings with Mark. Your position and contacts can play a critical part as you divide responsibilities.

Often there may be good reasons to take mutual responsibility for an action. If you want to demonstrate a "united front" with other teachers, for instance, you may decide to make a joint presentation to them. If one or both of you simply need the other's support, that too is an excellent reason for acting together, standing shoulder to shoulder, so to speak. Or you may simply enjoy collaborating—as in team teaching, for instance—taking pleasure in the mix of different styles, perspectives, and skills.

Finally, for the composing phase, we recommend a simple technique for dividing responsibilities. On a chalkboard or piece of newsprint, construct a matrix with these headings across the top: "Tasks," "Who?" "By When?" and "Resources Needed." List the tasks down the left side, and then decide together who will take on each task (either or both of you). Finally, agree on the deadlines by which each task will need to be done and any resources you will need, and fill out the matrix for each task. The reason for all this specificity and detail is that your continued collaboration (not to mention your relationship!) will depend to some degree on your individual and joint ability to follow through—to deliver, and in a timely way. Being absolutely clear together at this point will forestall confusion and other stresses in the future.

Following Through

Just as in the contracting phase, the mission and your continuing commitment to it and to one another keep showing up as colored strands in the fabric of your relationship. Working jointly or separately in the follow-through phase, you both are carrying out your joint mission. That means completing the tasks you have agreed to and sustaining the relationship.

Staying in Touch

Trusting one another to follow through, supporting one another, keeping track of developments and changes that may influence your project—all these needs suggest that *communicating frequently* remains the biggest task. You can compare notes with a quick word in the hall or with phone calls at night. People like Pam and Sarah, who see each other often, can take care of this informal updating easily and naturally. But others, like Meg and Mark, who have different workplaces and schedules, are likely to need more formal arrangements for keeping in touch: weekly check-ins by phone or a monthly meeting to take stock of Danny's progress and their own roles in working with the teachers. Whatever the mode, we encourage you to schedule regular connections as a way to ensure them despite the press of busy schedules.

Communication between partners during the action and follow-through benefit enormously from straight talk. As you both monitor your responses to events and to each other as a team, expressing your real opinion and talking directly to (not about!) your partner can help both of you to use your valuable time to deal with concerns important to you and your goals. For a review of the rules of straight talk, see Box 1.4 in Chapter 1.

Sharing Feedback

Giving and receiving feedback about your work together can help you to make major strides in your substantive work and, more important, to keep your relationship healthy. As Pam and Sarah, for example, clear their desks to write the final draft of their grant proposal, they could share feedback on how their talents and styles have helped get them as far as they have. Pam might ask, "How have my notes on hands-on science goals been helpful or unhelpful, Sarah, as you've drafted this section?" Sarah might observe, "I felt uncomfortable last night, Pam, wondering if you minded that I went and talked to the principal without you. Are you OK about that?" Or Pam might say more directly, "Sarah, I need to talk about something that's been bothering me about how we're doing," and then share how she felt when Sarah went to the principal without her. Feedback gives paired teams valuable information that allows them to adjust to one another and function better.

However, problems that feel more severe than Pam's and Sarah's can also arise in the course of following through. For whatever reason—incomplete contracting, a pattern of avoiding conflict, or stylistic differences that just seem too large to overcome—a pair can feel the relationship go sour. Because it is crucial to address this situation as early as possible, be aware of the "early warnings" that something needs your joint attention. You may find yourself worrying about the project and becoming angry at what feels like an imposition on you or a lack of responsibility in your partner, or you may suddenly realize that you are not looking forward to your next meeting. You may even have physical symptoms such as headaches, a churning stomach, or insomnia. Often the first inkling is about feeling burdened, carrying more than your fair share, and thinking it would be easier to carry on by yourself.

When that happens, feedback is the first recourse. Above all, as straight talk suggests (see Box 7.5, p. 122), we urge you not to talk to another person about the problem until you have discussed it with your partner. Although the discussion is likely to be difficult (you cannot expect your partner to be eager to hear what you will say!), it carries the hope of a new understanding and new agreements for your work together. The success of the conversation depends partly on your ability to state your perceptions and feelings without attacking your partner's motives or competence and partly on your partner's skills in hearing you and considering how to resolve the problem (see Box 3.5). Focusing strictly on the problematic *behavior* is crucial. The other guidelines for straight talk and our suggestions for framing your feedback can help you feel confident despite the discomfort of the situation (see Chapter 1, pp. 16-18).

If despite all your efforts you find yourselves at an impasse, we encourage you (as noted above in our suggestions about ground rules) to seek help from a third person—one who can take a neutral stance and help you sort through the dynamics of the conflict together. An outside consultant or another staff member skilled in mediation can help you recontract and reestablish your working relationship. Again, do not let these

---

Box 3.5
Suggestions for Receiving Feedback

1. Ask for feedback frequently—make it a normal, low-key way of working with others.

2. Make it safe and comfortable for others to give you feedback by

   - Accepting the information gracefully, not becoming defensive or hostile (or, if it is positive, not becoming overly modest and embarrassed)

   - Showing that you have heard the feedback and are willing to talk about the situation

3. Be willing to consider appropriate changes in your own behavior or roles and to develop new ground rules for your work together.

4. With unsolicited feedback that may be painful to hear, acknowledge your feelings and, when ready, focus with your partner on the behavior that has caused the problem. Try to see the feedback as an opportunity for recontracting; avoid, and ask your partner to avoid, an emphasis on blame and guilt.

troublesome situations build up into barriers that can seem insurmountable. Address them early while they are still manageable.

Finally, a word about your meetings. Generally, a working pair meets as often as needed to accomplish your task. Then, at some point, you face the possibility of closure, asking, "Are we finished? Have we completed our work on this project?" When that happens, we encourage you to have a final meeting to review all that you have been through together and to celebrate what you have accomplished. When a pair neglect this final step, they let the relationship slide away into a kind of oblivion rather than affirming the end of the project. Helping to avoid that way of ending, a final meeting is an essential way to honor your work and relationship with positive feedback to and from you both.

Facilitating Conditions

Paired teams have enormous potential for schools. Two people can form a productive team more easily than three or more. Two can more readily devise and carry out a plan, and they can more easily adjust to unforeseen circumstances than any other combination of adults. Here are a few environmental conditions that are essential to support paired teams.

- Regular times during the workday when teachers can contact other teachers, parents, or administrators to form and sustain paired teams
- Adult workspaces in schools to support research, planning, and the implementation of plans by pairs
- Phones, faxes, computers, and other communication systems to permit regular collaboration between partners (particularly with partners outside the school)
- A culture that supports the sharing of challenges and the formation of partnerships to create new solutions
- The services of qualified external and internal consultants who can help sort through conflicts and issues that pairs cannot resolve themselves
- Leaders who believe in collaborative solutions to learning problems and who will create opportunities for people to formulate

them (such as small innovative grants, staff development opportunities, and parent-teacher communications)

Resources

We have been unable to find a useful guide to action planning in pairs, but we recommend Friend and Cook's *Interactions: Collaboration Skills for School Professionals* (1992), Chapter 10, "Program Planning and Implementation."

Also helpful are two chapters from Blase and Blase's *Empowering Teachers: What Successful Principals Do* (1994), Chapter 2, "Trusting the Experts: Teachers," and Chapter 9, "Helping Solve Problems."

Resources on the identification of people's uniquenesses are widespread. Luft's *Of Human Interaction* (1969) describes clearly his Johari's Window schema for interpersonal communication. The standard work on the Myers-Briggs Type Indicator is Myers' *Gifts Differing* (1980). Two of the best secondary sources are Lawrence's *People Types and Tiger Stripes* (1982) and Kroeger's *Type Talk at Work* (1992).

On gender issues, especially communication, see Tannen's *You Just Don't Understand: Women and Men in Conversation* (1990). On the history and experiences of a variety of "minority" cultures in America, see Locke's *Increasing Multicultural Understanding: A Comprehensive Model* (1992). And for a resource book of activities designed to increase cultural awareness and cross-cultural sensitivity, see *Experiential Activities for Intercultural Learning*, edited by Seelye (1996).

References

Blase, J., & Blase, J. R. (1994). *Empowering teachers: What successful principals do.* Thousand Oaks, CA: Corwin.

Friend, M., & Cook, L. (1992). *Interactions: Collaboration skills for school professionals.* New York: Longman.

Kroeger, O. (1992). *Type talk at work.* New York: Delacorte.

Lawrence, G. D. (1982). *People types and tiger stripes* (2nd ed.). Gainesville, FL: CAPT, Inc.

Locke, D. C. (1992). *Increasing multicultural understanding: A comprehensive model.* Newbury Park, CA: Sage.

Luft, J. (1969). *Of human interaction.* Palo Alto, CA: National Press.

Myers, I. (1980). *Gifts differing.* Palo Alto, CA: Consulting Psychologists Press.

Seelye, H. N. (Ed.). (1996). *Experiential activities for intercultural learning.* Yarmouth, ME: Intercultural Press.

Tannen, D. (1990). *You just don't understand: Women and men in conversation.* New York: William Morrow.

PART II

Groups: Some Essential Features

In the next five chapters, we look at five different kinds of groups as they function in the life of schools. The first four are small groups: We imagine that they can contain as few as 3 and as many as 15 members, the most typical size ranging between 6 and 12. The fifth group, the faculty, can range in size from small to very large. All five groups—self-initiating groups, task committees, standing committees, working teams, and the faculty—play central roles in schools because they are the forums in which adults most often work together. Whether to develop an entirely new middle school curriculum, consider the problem of violence in school, plan this year's graduation ceremony, or team-teach the junior humanities curriculum, schools turn to these types of groups to accomplish the task.

As important as they are, it is ironic that committees and even some all-faculty events have developed a reputation as places for unproductive discussion and poor decisions. No doubt we all have served (or suffered!) on such groups, and our experiences have occasionally left us skeptical or even cynical about the chances for real collaboration. Experience and research, however, have demonstrated that groups, when nurtured with care and skill, offer extraordinary potential. They truly can become the vehicle of choice for handling many routine school tasks and virtually all efforts at innovation and reform. Just as important, they become manifestations of the spirit of a school—places for growth and learning, for enjoying work with one another, for the synergy that comes from high commitment to shared values and goals.

Although the various kinds of groups differ from each other in important ways, we preface the next five chapters by pointing out a principle and three lessons that apply to all groups. The principle is this: *When they are cared for, groups, much like individuals, mature in a transformational process that is essential to their productivity* (Napier & Gershenfeld, 1987). According to virtually all theories, groups have a substance and life of their own and, given certain conditions, they develop in somewhat predictable ways.

One model, developed and widely disseminated by the National Training Laboratories (NTL) Institute, sets out four stages of group development, roughly parallel to the infant, adolescent, middle-age, and elder stages of a person. In the *Reading Book for Human Relations Training* (Porter & Mohr, 1982, pp. 68-71), Richard C. Weber labels the stages in these rhyming terms: "Forming, Storming, Norming and Performing, and Transforming." The stages are not locked in a neat, linear progression; rather, they capture in a sequence the highly dynamic aspects of group life, and a group can occasionally move backward as it makes its journey through the various stages. Each stage, however, raises central issues for a group; if attended to, the issues are resolved, opening the way to the next stage, as follows:

1. *Infancy ("Forming").* The initial question for a new group is "What are we here for?" Membership and inclusion issues are paramount: "Do I belong here? Will I be accepted? Who are the others, and what are their intentions?" Ambiguity, uncertainty, and anxiety often mark this stage, and people are typically both nervous and "nice." People respond well to direction and support and usually welcome the chance to talk about purposes and expectations.

2. *Adolescence ("Storming").* The central issue here is power: "Can we agree to do this together? How much influence will I have?" Differences among members hold sway but are not tolerated well, let alone respected or revered; competition develops, and to a greater or lesser degree conflict makes this stage uniquely uncomfortable.

3. *Adulthood ("Norming and Performing").* "How shall we work together?" is the issue at this stage. With the question of power essentially resolved, the possibility of trust develops: "How will we function?" and "What special contributions can we each make?" Now the group is ready to work and do its work effectively.

4. *Elder Stage ("Transforming").* With its initial work accomplished, the group has to decide whether and/or how to continue as a group. A major question is "Shall we take on other tasks as a group?" The group either redefines its purpose or decides to disband.

Looking through a somewhat different lens at the life of groups, M. Scott Peck, in *The Different Drum: Community-Making and Peace* (1987), likewise sees four stages but emphasizes different qualities in each (see Box II.1). Peck wants to go beyond the "performance" of a work group; for him, a deep sense of community is the first goal of work groups, with "the love and commitment, the sacrifice, and the transcendence" required to build it (p. 108). Once having

---

Box II.1
The Four Stages of Community-Making

1. *Pseudo-Community.* As it forms, the group pretends it already has found community. It can do so only by ignoring the differences in the group, thus hoping to avoid conflict. Politeness is the (unspoken) rule.

2. *Chaos.* As the group allows differences to emerge, individuals struggle to abolish them by winning, choosing "right" and "wrong," converting each other, and getting nowhere. Conflict in this stage is uncreative and unproductive, yet members are beginning to open up and are no longer pretending.

3. *Emptiness.* As the bridge between chaos and community, "emptiness" signifies the transformational stage in which members let go of whatever has thus far kept the group from its real work: the preconceptions, prejudices, agendas, and other barriers to true communication that all members have brought to the group. Peck calls this action the group's "emotional surrender."

4. *Community.* This stage often begins with a sense of quiet peace. With genuine safety established, members feel free to be themselves, speaking and listening fully and authentically. The group is ready, at last, to work, to make decisions, to tackle solutions.

SOURCE: Adapted from Peck (1987).

attained that state, a group is ready to perform its ultimate task, the work for which it formed.

You will have seen by now that these models have influenced our own model's four stages of convening, contracting, composing, and following through. For us, as for Weber and Peck in different degrees, each stage of a group's development must focus both on the "outer" work or mission of the group and on its "inner" work: the relationships among its members, including the attitudes people bring to one another, the way they behave together, the quality of their skills, and so on. Thus *the first major lesson of group development theory is that focusing exclusively on the group's stated mission courts disaster.* The spirit of the group needs nurturing, initially most of all, and it develops best in tandem with the outer work as members explore their differences and struggle to create a shared purpose.

A second lesson is that *conflict is a natural part of group life and development.* Early in the life of a group (the "storming" or "chaos" stage), conflict is an inevitable and normal, if not especially pleasant, condition. Only through the discomforts and fights, the fits and false starts that characterize the second stage, can the group confront and discover its essential strength—the differences that members bring to the group. The healthiness of this conflict is captured in the maxim "Differentiation precedes integration": A group develops only by recognizing the separateness and differences among its members.

Later, having learned how to honor and capitalize on those differences, the group handles conflict in a much different way. The magic of a mature group is that it views conflict as helpful to its task. A new or different opinion, a second thought, a sudden concern—these become a necessary part of the work, and group members treat them as essential contributions.

A final, related lesson: *Mature groups develop their remarkable cohesiveness, interdependence, and effectiveness by fully using all individual members' gifts.* In the latter stages of development, a crucial task for group members is to discover what skills they can offer for the good of the group. Some of these skills are operational or logistical, such as setting agendas, note taking, and monitoring of follow-through activities. Other skills emerge as members work together, sensing what the group needs and acting to meet the need. In *Redesigning Collegiate Leadership: Teams and Teamwork in Higher Education* (1993), Estela Mara Bensimon and Anna Neumann identified and described in detail eight roles that contribute to successful groups. (Because various group members can play these "roles," we prefer to think of them as clusters of skills.) The idea is that these skills profoundly influence the group by drawing others into a total group action. As shown in Box II.2, the first five skills represent the "core of team thinking," and the last three "support, facilitate, maintain, and redirect the work of this core" (p. 60).

Bensimon and Neumann make it clear that any member may display several skills. The breadth of the five core skills shows how many kinds of mental processes go into "thinking" and why mature groups, using their wide array of talents, are capable of results that an individual cannot accomplish alone. The supporting skills demonstrate in part the importance of staying aware of *how* the group is working. The skills of checking on task and emotions often lead to the kinds of interventions we note in discussing the "bedrock skills" (see Chapter 1), as members call attention to the group's work proc-

---

Box II.2
Eight Skills for Successful Groups

Core Skills:

- *Defining:* Articulating a view of the group's situation and context and thus helping to create the group's reality.
- *Analyzing:* Examining issues already defined (e.g., assessing components of a problem)
- *Interpreting:* Translating how people outside the group are likely to understand the issues
- *Critical thinking:* Offering redefinition, reanalysis, or reinterpretation of the group's issues
- *Synthesizing:* Eliciting diverse thinking roles, building a sense of reality for the group to act on

Supporting Skills:

- *Awareness of the task:* Trying to remove obstacles to group thinking and facilitating the group's processes generally
- *Awareness of emotions:* Helping to establish and maintain the human, personal, and emotional context within which the group operates
- *Awareness of disparities:* Once the group takes action, assessing how people outside the group in fact make sense of the group's actions

SOURCE: Adapted from Bensimon and Neumann (1993, p. 59).

---

esses, values, emotional states, and internal relationships. This eight-skill model, by pointing out the many needs of a group, underscores the paradoxical lesson that a group becomes most cohesive and productive when its individual members are most fully involved in using their own special—and different—gifts.

With the developmental nature of groups as background, we turn now to the most typical forms of group collaboration in schools. In each of the next five chapters, we discuss a particular kind of group. Our aim is to help you and your colleagues discover approaches and activities that will accomplish two things in your work together: nurturing the development of your school groups and carrying out group tasks for the good of the school and its students.

References

Bensimon, E. M., & Neumann, A. (1993). *Redesigning collegiate leadership: Teams and teamwork in higher education.* Baltimore: Johns Hopkins University Press.

Napier, R., & Gershenfeld, M. (1987). *Groups: Theory and experience.* Boston: Houghton Mifflin.

Peck, M. S. (1987). *The different drum: Community-making and peace.* New York: Simon & Schuster.

Weber, R. C. (1982). The group: A cycle from birth to death. In L. Porter & B. Mohr (Eds.), *Reading book for human relations training* (pp. 68-71). Arlington, VA: NTL Institute.

4

We Could Do It Together!
The Self-Initiating Group

It was 4:10 p.m. on a November day. Six faculty members sat around a conference table at Sherwood High. For the past 45 minutes, they'd been deep in discussion about what they termed "the lost sophomores." The group had assembled rather spontaneously following a conversation between Sid, a counselor, and Connie, a "sophomore" English teacher.

Sid's and Connie's initial concern was that too many sophomores became disaffected at Sherwood High and eventually dropped out. As they struggled to keep a few kids from becoming "lost," they included others in their conversations: Ted, a unified arts teacher; Sarah, a math teacher; Chloe, a social studies teacher; and Fran, a vice principal. They had been talking informally now for about 6 weeks.

"I really like your idea, Ted," Connie was saying. "We could predict who these kids are going to be, even as early as eighth grade. Then we'd be prepared to get them into the right classes before they went sour on school."

"I agree," Chloe chimed in. "But I don't think it's enough to just identify them early. We've got to do what Sarah and Sid were talking about last week: Build a whole curriculum for them."

"Yeah! I'm more and more frustrated as I work with these kids," Sid said, "because ultimately I'm counseling them to stay in classes with subjects and teachers that they've already failed at. Sometimes the teachers have written them off, too."

Fran, the vice principal, added, "I know what you mean, Sid. I'm often doing the same thing with those 15 or 20 kids we've been talking about. You know, I think this is a great project for the board's new Competitive Advantage Fund. I'll bet we could put together a small proposal and buy ourselves the time to plan something for next year to pick these kids up."

"You serious, Fran? I had no idea there was such a fund," Connie said. "What do you all think?"

This snapshot of a small group of concerned educators might have come from any school, from any day in the school year. Whenever teachers, counselors, administrators, and parents have the chance to talk, their conversation often turns to what they can do better for their students and children. In this instance, the group's concern has sprung from a shared challenge. A set of students they all work with is clearly not benefiting from the school as it should. These six educators have managed to sustain a conversation among themselves about these kids. Now, an opportunity has presented itself—the Competitive Advantage Fund—that will allow them to work more systematically on their ideas.

The Sherwood High group is a self-initiating group. From its beginnings in offhand conversations prompted by a common need, it has the potential to develop into a working group that can make a big difference at Sherwood. At this point, early in its life, the group is bonded together by each individual's sense of the importance of helping "lost sophomores." If all these individuals can form themselves successfully into a working group for this purpose, they can have extraordinary power to create solutions that can transform the curriculum and culture of the sophomore year at Sherwood.

In this chapter, we explore the dynamics at work in such self-initiating groups.

Convening

Self-initiating groups grow naturally from repeated conversation and opportunities to mingle. For this reason, their starting point is frequently difficult to pinpoint. Nobody necessarily calls a formal meeting to convene the group. Rather, it evolves as people identify a need or goal and find that others whom they like and respect seem to share this need or goal. The great strength of these self-initiating groups lies in the voluntary nature of membership as members convene around commonly felt needs. People are in the working group because they want to be and believe in its purpose.

Some of these groups never move beyond the conversational level, yet still serve useful functions. For example, teachers who share the same lunch break or a principal and a group of teachers who habitually arrive at school early and have coffee and talk together have not made a conscious choice as a group to accomplish some end. Nevertheless, by virtue of their continued gathering in a voluntary way, they serve some important function for one another. This function could be nearly anything—to lend moral support, to share information about students or teaching, to enjoy friendship, to complain, and to catch up on news from yesterday. These groups share unspoken covenants; they convene because they are useful to their members and do not often need to be any more formal about their purposes or ground rules than that. Self-initiating groups are extraordinarily important ways for educators to feel affiliated with one another and for information (accurate or not!) to spread around a busy school.

Some self-initiating groups, however, find that they need to "form" in a more formal sense. As in our scenario, some members recognize the potential for accomplishing a more discrete goal, such as writing a grant application to address the "lost sophomore" problem. The group is beginning to discuss a more public purpose and to take on the form of a task-oriented team. At this point, we suggest that you be particularly careful with one another. You are suggesting a change in the already existing "informal" compact that defines a relatively limited membership and permits loose rules and agendas. All members might not choose to commit to this new focus or to wider membership and action.

For this reason, we suggest that you think of the convening stage as exploratory in three respects and that the group actually discuss these repeatedly. First, think of your discussions about purpose as a process of identifying, from all the issues and ideas you have been talking about, one or two problems or opportunities that the group can realistically tackle.

Second, look at your discussions as a chance to ensure that a variety of interested people and different perspectives are included in the group. In our experience, such a deliberate "search for diversity" can be difficult to *want* to do because it goes against the grain. After all, the group has probably convened around established relationships and friendships, shared viewpoints, and a common history; it has a natural comfort that resists being disturbed. In the long run, though, the group's success will almost certainly depend on its inclusiveness and its ability to honor different backgrounds and viewpoints. So we encourage you to ask the question, "Who's not here? What interests, backgrounds, resources, and other talents do we need to tackle this issue?" In that way, you help to ensure that valuable new members are included in your group—perhaps to achieve gender balance, to include members of other races, or to involve a parent.

Finally, think of your discussions as ways to test out each member's willingness to commit to working together on these problems. It is especially important to give one another room to withdraw or explore alternative roles in the group; the key ingredient of a well-functioning self-initiating team is that membership is voluntary. If you can talk about these three things—the group's purpose, its diversity, and people's willingness to be in the group and to work toward the purpose—you will have convened a special group, "custom-made" for the particular task you have each committed to explore together.

Contracting

Let us assume that the self-initiating group has convened on a somewhat more formal basis than it had earlier. You are probably just where Sid and Connie were when they asked the other teachers and the vice principal to join them. Each of you has a rough idea of the group's purpose (e.g., "to do something to help the 'lost sophomores' "), and you probably know one another to differing degrees. The first and most important task is *not* to brainstorm solutions to the problem (although that is where many groups try to begin). Rather, the members must agree to *form the group itself*; the task is to deepen your knowledge of each other and decide how you want to work together *before* you plunge into the task.

Think of this first step as having two goals: to create a climate in which all members are valued for who they are and what they bring to the group (the relationship dimension) and to develop a shared sense of mission (the task dimension). We suggest you begin by becoming better acquainted, in the context of your work as educators and the situation facing the group (see Box 4.1). Turning then to the mission, you might explore together whatever situation has brought you together. The idea is not so much to "write a mission statement" as to ask, "How do we each see this problem?" or "What are our experiences about this situation?" Both questions invite everyone to contribute stories and opinions and help to lay a level field for all members, new and old.

The second major task of contracting is to negotiate members' expectations of each other and the operational roles they will play. With the typical informality and enthusiasm of a self-initiating group, members might fall naturally into a certain role ("I'll take notes this time"). We encourage you to make the negotiations explicit, however, by discussing specific needs the group will face, making working agreements, and writing them down as "ground rules." Consider these essential questions that every group faces:

- How will we record our meetings?
- How will we manage time?
- How will we ensure open communication among us all?
- How will we handle conflict?
- How will we make decisions?
- Who will lead our group?
- How will we communicate with the rest of the school?

Box 4.1
"Who We Are": A Self-Disclosure Activity

If members do not know each other very well, focusing on yourselves as individuals helps to establish the group on a solid footing of personal knowledge. This simple activity offers each member in turn a 15-minute period in which to tell how he or she came to be "the person I am today" in whatever way the person chooses. There are only two rules:

1. As each one speaks, others are just to listen.
2. If a speaker stops talking with time to spare, others have the chance to ask questions until the time is up.

Although it takes some time, the activity creates a common bond for members that pays dividends later on.

Box 4.2
Ground Rules: A Sample

Agreeing on ground rules works best when members have the chance to suggest some of their own. This list suggests some possibilities:

- Listen carefully to each other.
- Only one person talks at a time.
- Test underlying assumptions and inferences.
- Share all relevant information.
- Be specific—use examples.
- Give the reasons for what you say and do.
- Make statements, then invite questions and comments.
- Disagree openly with anyone in the group.
- Discuss undiscussable issues.
- Keep the discussion focused.
- Don't take cheap shots; avoid put-downs.
- Participate fully.

SOURCE: Adapted from Schwarz (1994).

Agreeing on ground rules focuses on members' expectations and behavior *before* the group has developed very far. In terms of the stages of group development described earlier, the group deliberately creates the "norming" stage near the outset of its development, before conflicts arise, and thus builds a foundation that will help the group manage the inevitable conflicts to come. Later, when difficulties arise during the group's composing work (as they will!), you can remind each other of these early agreements. Boxes 4.2 and 4.3 offer sample sets of ground rules that groups have found useful as a starting point. Ground rules give you the chance to name disruptive or troublesome behaviors in terms that all members have helped to create, and to do so descriptively rather than judgmentally.

A final consideration in contracting is the group's relationship to others in school. Unlike an appointed task committee or standing committee, the self-initiating group begins with no official status or mandate, and depending on the situation, that condition can be either a help or a hindrance. As the group gains a more specific sense of purpose and begins to think about some kind of action, others are likely to want to know what you are "up to." It is best, of course, if you tell them about your intentions before they ask, so early on it may be wise to inform the principal and perhaps the whole faculty and seek their support.

The contracting phase typically results in a clearer sense of the situation you want to address, deeper commitments to a shared

purpose, greater appreciation of members' differences
and commonalities, and
some important public
agreements about how you
want to work together. Next
comes the phase in which
all the discussions thus far
begin to move toward decisions and action.

Composing

Sid, Connie, and the
others in the "lost sophomores" group are just be-
ginning to work on the proposal Fran suggested they
write for the board's Competitive Advantage Fund.

> **Box 4.3**
> **The "Full-Value Contract"**
>
> We agree to
> 1. Create and participate in a group
>   that is physically and emotionally
>   safe
> 2. Work together to achieve
>   individual and group goals
> 3. Give and receive honest feedback
> 4. Guard against devaluing ourselves
>   and try our best to change this
>   behavior
> 5. Let go of negative thoughts and
>   feelings and be willing to move on
>   in the processes of learning,
>   growth, and relationships
>
> SOURCE: Adapted from *Training Manuals on Teamwork*,
> Project Adventure, Hamilton, MA. Used with permission.

As a more formal self-initiating group, well on its way to maturity,
what approach might it take and what tasks might it take on? For this
kind of group, we suggest an approach that optimizes the members'
enthusiasm by challenging them to discover new opportunities (rather
than to solve problems). As to the tasks, we propose five, as follows:

- Assessing the current situation
- Visioning
- Action planning
- Affirming members' commitment to the action plans
- Acquiring institutional commitment

Assessing the Current Situation

In *The Path of Least Resistance* (1989), Robert Fritz demonstrated
that by placing a clear picture of current reality next to an equally clear
picture or vision of what we truly want, we identify the gap between
what we have and what we want. He argued that when we see the

gap, our natural tendency is to move toward making the vision real. Fritz's work suggests how groups can benefit from assessing the current situation and then creating a vision of what they really want.

The goal of assessing where things stand now is to create a full and accurate picture of today's reality and a shared understanding of the forces that have caused it. In the 6 weeks that Sid's and Connie's group has been meeting, for example, it is likely that they have pretty well informally assessed the current situation for the "lost sophomores." A little more formally, the group can assess the current situation by asking, first, "What's working well?" and then, "What's working poorly?" Thinking about both positive and negative aspects of today's reality can produce a comprehensive picture, including current strategies that are working well but may be limited or need strengthening. The exercise itself is simple. Every member has the chance to contribute to the assessment, and capturing the list of perceptions on a chalkboard or newsprint allows the group to come back to specific items for further discussion. After clarifying the specifics, the group turns to discovering patterns and themes among all the perceptions, leading to generalizations that are likely to be more accurate because they rely on the whole group's insights.

Visioning

Though appropriate for virtually all working groups, visioning is especially fitting for a self-initiating group because it almost always unifies people. Scarcely any other group event captures, intensifies, and focuses members' energy for a task better than a vision. Coming near the beginning of the composing phase, it also offers a positive, forward-looking approach to a set of often complex tasks.

Visioning answers the question, "About this subject, what do we truly want to see in the future?" A vision uniquely blends our hopes for the future with images of what that future might actually look like. When a group responds to such a question, its members tap into their deepest desires, beliefs, and values about the subject and create an actual or verbal picture of what they want to achieve. Thus a vision represents a preferred future, a desired state, and—the crux of it—*a leap from where things stand today.*

Your visioning needs to focus on the situation you seek to improve. The goal is to create the equivalent for your group of "sophomores no longer lost." It is best not to place too many constraints on a visioning process. Imagine a time far enough ahead to allow real change to have taken place. Think about the people who will be involved and how they work together; imagine their activities, their successes, the impacts of innovative policies, the quality and means of communication, leadership issues and styles, buildings and facilities—innovations of all sorts. A few guidelines (see Box 4.4) are usually enough to move the group into productive and often stimulating work.

One way of visioning is to depict your group's preferred future graphically with markers, construction paper, and other materials. A highlight of this technique is that members often express their vision in organic images—flowers, trees, plants, hearts, and so on—portraying dynamic, living, growing systems. In another approach, the group compiles a list of visionary items, including images, ideas, causes and effects—a hodgepodge that needs refining. The group distills the crucial elements of its vision, reframing them into a short list that captures the shared desires of the group. If one element does not receive everyone's approval and the conflict cannot be resolved, separate the disputed element from the rest because it is not part of the shared vision. The biggest challenge in refining the vision is to keep the specificity and the sense of excitement of the original brainstorming. Concentrating on images—on what people actually *see* for the future—can help.

The vision serves as the group's guiding star, showing the place the group wants to go. It has another important use: When a group is writing a proposal or report, as Sid's and Connie's group is, the vision can become a part of the document, showing funders and other readers exactly what the proposal wants to create. And that brings us to the next step: Now the group can consider how to realize its vision.

Box 4.4
Guidelines for Visioning

1. Focus on what you truly want, not on how to get there.
2. For now, don't worry about what you think is possible.
3. Focus on what you want, not on avoiding what you don't want.
4. Make choices for yourself and your group—not for others.
5. If you use words, express the vision in the present tense (e.g., "We are" rather than "We will be").
6. If you are drawing images, work for shared, cohesive images or symbols that communicate vividly.

SOURCE: Adapted from correspondence with Michael Brazzel, a consultant colleague in Columbia, MD.

Action Planning

Following the maxim that "if you don't know where you're going, you're likely to end up somewhere else," action planning usually begins with setting goals. The vision is helpful here because implicitly it contains the long-term goals the group wants to pursue. You may want to set short-term goals that will allow you to focus on the weeks and months just ahead. Box 4.5 outlines the essentials of action planning: identifying short-term goals and barriers to them, identifying alternative strategies to reach those goals, then planning specific actions to realize a plausible strategy for the group.

> **Box 4.5**
> **Goals, Strategies, and Action Plans**
>
> 1. What are our goals?
> 2. What are the major barriers standing in the way of the goals?
> 3. What alternative strategies would help to overcome the barriers?
> 4. What actions need to be taken to move ahead?
>   a. Who will be responsible for each one?
>   b. When do the actions need to be taken?
>   c. How (resources needed)?

Working through these steps, give special attention to two areas. First, when the group considers what strategies to pursue, the danger is to think too narrowly and decide too quickly on one or two strategies. The technique of brainstorming helps. By generating all kinds of alternative strategies, the group expands its thinking and considers creative options before deciding on a single path. We encourage you to review the rules of brainstorming together (see Box 4.6).

The crucial point in using this technique is to create a sense of safety so that everyone can express whatever comes up and so that all ideas, feelings, and possibilities—no matter how apparently wild they may seem to other members—are welcome. (This helps to overcome the major weakness with this method of brainstorming, which is that it does not guarantee everyone an equal level of participation; for a technique that does that, see Chapter 6, p. 102.) Keep in mind that the principle behind brainstorming is that *creating* ideas works best if kept separated from the process of *evaluating* them. Critical thinking skills come to the fore later when the group reviews the brainstormed alternatives and selects those that seem best.

Second, it is most helpful to be as specific as possible when identifying "next-step" actions. When your group is discussing action steps, they are often first described as fairly general tactics. So that everyone has the same understanding of "next steps," these need to be discussed until each step is a discrete action with "who, when, and how" specified. For instance: "Share with rest of faculty" might become either "Put on next faculty meeting agenda" or "Ted and Ann send memo to all teachers by next Friday."

> **Box 4.6**
> **Brainstorming**
>
> 1. Bring up as many ideas as possible. Record them in view of all.
> 2. No remarks, criticism, reactions! Everyone calls out ideas, and no one judges them.
> 3. Do not censor yourself. Express your ideas even if they seem farfetched and even if you doubt them.
> 4. Encourage everyone to participate (to help ensure that all are involved).
> 5. Make it fun, and keep it lively. It helps to set a time limit for brainstorming. Often there is a short lull, followed by renewed energy and a new burst of ideas.
> 6. After all ideas have surfaced, evaluate, combine, and organize them.

Affirming Members' Commitment to the Plan

Just as testing commitment to the mission is important in the convening phase, testing and reaffirming everyone's continuing dedication is crucial to the composing phase. It is helpful for all members to develop ways to demonstrate their approval (or not) as the group sets goals, considers alternative strategies, and identifies actions. Conversely, members can question each other at various points: "Are we all together on this decision?" or "Before we decide, let's be sure we've thought it through. Any doubts?" The composing phase includes critical decisions, and if the group overlooks one member's sudden silence or apparent withdrawal and plunges on without ensuring full support, the moment will return to haunt everyone sooner or later.

As you near the end of the composing phase, it is important to attach members' names to each action, agree on dates for completion, and list any needed resources (see Chapter 3, p. 49, for a simple technique for action planning). There are two reasons for this. First, taking responsibility in this way helps to ensure that things will really happen, and happen on time (the group might also discuss how to handle communications if agreements cannot be honored later on). Second, the technique lets members think together about their talents and capacities for taking on different tasks and volunteer for those that make good sense individually and for the group. As always, we encourage you to talk about these questions openly and candidly, negotiating with clarity about each other's abilities and needs.

Acquiring Institutional Commitment

Finally, some self-initiating groups may need to check back with school leaders to ensure institutional commitment to the plan. Remember, principals do not like some kinds of surprises! Checking back is partly a question of timing. With Sid's and Connie's group, for instance, the principal is likely to want to see the complete proposal in draft form before supporting it, and so the group should put off this step until near the end of its work. But another group, working, let us say, on a new staff development program, would have used the composing phase to design the program, and now would find it crucial to gain the institution's commitment before moving on to implementation. In short, the question is situational, with each group deciding for itself. Be sure to raise the question together, however, to gain needed resources, approval, permission, or protection, or simply to be sure that you will not surprise school leaders and others later on.

Following Through

If a group's work concludes with a proposal, report, or recommendation, the follow-through can be relatively brief. Implementing the plan is largely a matter of writing up and reporting the group's work, and the group may meet just once or twice in this phase to review together a draft of the proposal, meet with the principal, and celebrate its initial work.

But if a group's action plan extends into implementing a grant or a set of recommendations, following through becomes a longer, more complex phase in which all the members may have a variety of tasks to accomplish in a coordinated way. The commitments members made in the action-planning steps at the end of the composing phase become especially important now. The group's attention to communication and trust amongst its members and, eventually, to closure will often spell the difference between success and failure.

Communication and Trust

During follow-through, the quality of the group's norms and expectations of one another (built up deliberately through the earlier phases) is really tested. Because much of the action is mutual and simultaneous now, and because it is often public in this phase, the group's success depends on the level of trust and communication among group members. Formal meetings may be less frequent, yet members need to check in with one another, in pairs or larger subgroups, reporting on progress and setbacks. Each member feels responsible for his or her part, *and* everyone looks for ways to help and support other members as the need arises. Revisiting the ground rules together can help sustain this sense of shared responsibility in action.

Returning to our scenario, imagine the group's work once it has obtained the planning grant. Let us say that the action plan called for the whole group to meet with all the 10th-grade teachers and then for three members to talk with a number of the "lost" students before designing a block of special sophomore courses. Meanwhile, Connie and Sid must talk to the principal about available resources for the new courses, and the principal must have time to check with the superintendent and board. As these activities take place, the entire group does not meet all the time, but individuals and the working subgroups must stay in close touch with each other and with the rest of the group. This means everything from quick, unscheduled conversations in the hall, to evening phone calls, to scheduled weekly memos from Sid and Connie.

Now too is the time for giving and asking for feedback. Giving positive feedback is especially important (and often overlooked) in this phase. It is easy to say to ourselves, for instance, "Sid said he'd do it, and then he did it—no big deal!" But this kind of accomplishment is just what the group needs and exists for, so (besides the effect it can have on Sid himself) appreciating Sid's work "out loud" marks an important milestone for the group. It says, in effect, "We're doing significant things here, we're doing them well, and we continue to care about each other."

The other major reason for staying in close contact with one another during follow-through is so the group can monitor progress and revise its plan as necessary. Complex plans almost always require adjustments and modifications in their implementation. Revisions will be needed as external circumstances change or the group itself changes; either way, members may need to call the group together for changes in action plans and perhaps even in strategy.

Closure

Many groups pay no heed to the important business of closure. They simply dissolve, members drifting off in June as if the tasks were everything and their relationships nothing. The final meetings of a self-initiating group are exceptionally important; they offer everyone the chance to reflect on the group's accomplishments, celebrate each person's hard work, and close the group. Our first suggestion here is this: Be sure to hold a closing meeting!

If possible, hold this meeting at an informal site that allows for celebration, and be sure that all members have a chance to speak from their hearts to the rest of the group. This is an important time to appreciate each one's contribution to the effort and offer special thanks to the group's leaders. This is also the time to look ahead, agreeing on what will happen next. Will this group reconvene around another task? If so, will there be changes in membership? These may be difficult questions, but they are important "bookends" to the commitments members made to one another during convening and contracting. If handled well, closure will encourage you and your colleagues to form other self-initiating groups to accomplish future goals for your school.

Facilitating Conditions

Self-initiating groups form on their own, often outside the influence of administration and formal structures. You could even say that they form despite (or sometimes in opposition to) leadership's intentions. Because self-initiating groups have such potential for improving schools, however, we urge principals, superintendents, school boards, and teacher leaders to encourage and nurture such groups. Their active facilitation can funnel the energy and commitment of these groups toward goals and activities that enhance the entire school.

To this end, we suggest

- Scheduling regular opportunities for faculty to gather for conversation about perceived needs in the school—these are opportunities for self-initiating groups to germinate
- Providing time, space, information, resources, and encouragement for self-initiating groups to meet
- Resisting the urge to discourage such groups because they appear to "have a cause" or to be creating more work for everyone
- Keeping communications open to faculty and administration and making their efforts part of the school's legitimate professional activity
- Providing avenues for the goals and action plans of self-initiating groups to be implemented at first on a pilot basis and, if they prove productive, on a more widespread scale
- Celebrating the initiative of the group members and spreading the news of their efforts to help the school

Resources

For the importance and use of ground rules, a guide to action planning, and a treatment of most other aspects of working with task groups, a place to start is Schwarz's *The Skilled Facilitator: Practical Wisdom for Developing Effective Groups* (1994). Though aimed primarily at group facilitators, the book is useful as well for group members. A resource intended more directly for groups of educators is Miles's *Learning to Work in Groups* (1981). Goodman offers a useful array of ideas in *Designing Effective Work Groups* (1986).

For resources on and assistance with experiential approaches to team building, contact Project Adventure, P.O. Box 100, Hamilton, MA 01936 (the source for the Full-Value Contract concept).

To help with vision building with your colleagues, see *Creating New Visions for Schools: Activities for Educators, Parents, and Community Members*, by the Regional Laboratory for the Educational Improvement of the Northeast and Islands (1994). For the theory behind visioning, see Fritz's *The Path of Least Resistance* (1989). On the process of visioning, many helpful sources exist. Nanus has devoted an entire book to the arts and techniques of *Visionary Leadership: Creating a Compelling Sense of Direction for Your Organization* (1992).

For practical techniques to help your group with problem solving and planning, see Arbuckle and Murray's *Building Systems for Professional Growth: An Action Guide* (1989). An excellent source on visioning and action planning is *The Fifth Discipline Fieldbook: Strategies and Tools for Building a Learning Organization*, by Senge, Kleiner, Roberts, Ross, and Smith (1994).

References

Arbuckle, M., & Murray, L. (1989). *Building systems for professional growth: An action guide.* Andover, MA: Regional Laboratory for Educational Improvement of the Northeast and Islands.

Fritz, R. (1989). *The path of least resistance.* New York: Fawcett Columbine.

Goodman, P. (1986). *Designing effective work groups.* San Francisco: Jossey-Bass.

Miles, M. (1981). *Learning to work in groups* (2nd ed.). New York: Teachers College Press.

Nanus, B. (1992). *Visionary leadership: Creating a compelling sense of direction for your organization.* San Francisco: Jossey-Bass.

Regional Laboratory for the Educational Improvement of the Northeast and Islands. (1994). *Creating new visions for schools: Activities for educators, parents, and community members.* Andover, MA: Author.

Schwarz, R. M. (1994). *The skilled facilitator: Practical wisdom for developing effective groups.* San Francisco: Jossey-Bass.

Senge, P., Kleiner, A., Roberts, C., Ross, R. B., & Smith, B. J. (1994). *The fifth discipline fieldbook: Strategies and tools for building a learning organization.* New York: Doubleday.

5

Appoint a Committee to Handle It!

The Task Committee

As Steve pulled into his parking spot at Sedomak Junior High, he thought forward to his afternoon meeting. It had been 5 months since Mario, their principal, had appointed Steve and Doris to co-chair a New Standards Committee consisting of six other teachers. Of late, it seemed to Steve that they had become bogged down. When Mario had given them their charge to designate "minimum achievement standards" in the basic skills, it had seemed so clear. But now the whole project seemed so complicated, and time (and energy) was so short. They had 2 more months to get their recommendations approved by the faculty and presented to the school board.

Today's meeting, Steve feared, was going to be like last week's. Doris, Jamaal, and Larry had been assigned to bring a draft of "essential math skills" for Grades 7 and 8 to share with the committee. The rest of the group would read them over, and Geneva and Lonnie would undoubtedly suggest alternatives. The discussion would focus on one or two skill areas and probably come to a halt over the wording that Doris, Jamaal, and Larry used. Steve just hoped that Doris would not slide into defensiveness about the draft as she had last week.

As Steve entered the building, Mario greeted him, and they exchanged pleasantries. Then Mario asked, "Say, the Standards Committee is meeting this afternoon, isn't it?"

Steve reported that it was and took the opportunity to share his growing concern about the project. "You know, Mario, I'm getting worried about our progress. We're meeting every week for 3 hours, but we're not coming to a consensus very fast. We've spent all our time just drafting lists of essential skills, and it seems like we're just beginning to agree when people get hung up about wording or one little skill."

"I was wondering about that myself, Steve. Larry mentioned something to me last night. He was frustrated that Geneva and Lonnie never seem satisfied with what's going on."

"Yeah, I know. I think they've got quite a different idea about what the New Standards should be used for. They're worried they'll be rammed down our throats by the school board and even that they'll become a way to evaluate each of us as teachers."

"What's your deadline on the committee, Steve? Two or 3 months?"

"March 15—just about 2 months from today. I think you and Doris and I should get together and talk about it."

Steve, Doris and their colleagues find themselves in a position increasingly familiar to educators everywhere. Site-based management and school improvement initiatives have spawned a colorful offspring of task forces, special committees, and study groups. These are usually convened formally by administration or faculty to accomplish a specific purpose by a certain date. Membership is either voluntary, assigned by the convening authority, or a combination of the two. Task committees are expected to deliver a product to the faculty, the administration, or the board that reflects research, thought, planning, and the opinions of multiple constituencies. By assigning important tasks to special groups, the institution is presumably mobilizing its resources in the most efficient manner.

The Sedomak Junior High story illustrates some of the complications that accompany the task committee strategy. As familiar as this story is to many of us, it points out the need to understand better how task committees can support authentic collaboration.

Convening

Unlike the pairs and groups we have discussed in previous chapters, the task committee has a formal beginning. Someone literally convenes it by defining its purpose and appointing its members. This process is often rather perfunctory and is usually conducted by the administration. But it is very important to the future success of the group, as it defines not only what the group is to do but its time line and the rationale for its membership.

The "convener," whether the principal, superintendent, the school board, the faculty leadership, or the faculty as a whole, needs to be aware of the importance of explaining the committee's background and purpose to both the committee and the faculty. What is the situation or problem to be addressed? What has led to this committee's formation? The clearer the convener can be with everyone, the more likely the committee will be to start on the right foot. The convener can cover these four key points in presenting the committee with its charge:

1. *Mission:* Explain the committee's mission and how it will serve the school and its students.
2. *Role:* Define the committee's role and authority in relation to the rest of the school, specifying the expected outcome and whether it is to be general advice, a recommendation, or a definitive decision.
3. *Schedule:* Describe projected time lines for the committee's work, including intermediate checkpoints and the end point when its product is due.
4. *Membership:* Explain who the members are and the rationale for selecting them (for example, on the basis of expertise, representativeness, interest, future ownership, first-come-first-appointed, open-to-all).

All members of the committee should have the opportunity to discuss these *at the outset* with the convener and among themselves so they understand their charge and the parameters surrounding it. An example of a "charge" statement can be found in Box 5.1. The rest of the school's staff also needs to understand the task committee's purpose, role, schedule, and membership.

Box 5.1
The Committee's Charge: An Example

The purpose of the New Standards Committee is to recommend for faculty and board approval the minimum achievement standards in the basic skills at each grade level for Sedomak Junior High School students. For the committee's purposes, the basic skills include writing, reading, math, physical abilities, and citizenship. The larger goal is to raise and enhance the quality of education at Sedomak by setting clear, supportable standards for grade promotion.

Because the board's intention is to employ these standards in the next academic year, the committee must develop its initial recommendations for faculty review by March 15.

Committee members include Doris Miller and Steve Callatino as cochairs, Jamaal Abtaruk, Lonnie Andrews, Geneva Critchland, Jennifer Fugate, Larry McMahon, and Linda Martin. Members have been appointed on the basis of availability and interest in the subject, and to balance representation by gender, race, ethnicity, and grade level.

Groups of this type are sometimes cloaked in mystery. Others seem unclear about what the committee is to do or why some people are members and others are not. The work of these groups can bog down in this mystery, and mistrust can grow. When task groups are convened, and even before they are, those individuals and groups who will be affected by the committee's work must know what is going on and how the committee's work might affect them.

As the task committee is convened, both the convener and the committee itself can share the committee's charge and membership criteria with the staff and appropriate groups outside the school. Anticipate these kinds of common questions: Will the committee make decisions that will limit my choices as a teacher? Will the committee report to the board and bypass the faculty? Will the committee and the principal write a proposal that will bring resources to some staff and not to others? Because the members of the group might be exercising authority even indirectly over others, who they are and how they were chosen can be significant to the faculty and staff. Openness about these choices—and considering the option of making membership open to all—will dispel doubt and forestall internal and external politicking.

Contracting

When the convener and committee members manage the convening phase carefully, they also complete several critical aspects of contracting by agreeing on a written mission statement, the group's goals, and a date for completing the task. The group's first meeting, after it meets with the convener, is usually the best time for this crucial contracting activity.

The first goal of contracting is to test and ensure each member's commitment to the group's purpose, and it often requires extended discussion to reach the clarity that people may need. In our scenario of the New Standards Committee, well into their work (in fact, just 2 months from the principal's deadline), Geneva and Lonnie are blocking the group's progress because of their fears about the school board's intentions. This is just the kind of problem that good contracting can forestall. What is required is careful, direct description of the group's purpose (written and oral) and some encouragement for committee members to raise hopes, questions, and fears.

But let us say that Mario, the principal, in convening the New Standards Committee, did not write a charge and discuss it with the group; he simply gave Steve, the chair, an idea of what he wanted, told him who the members were, and asked Steve to proceed to get the committee together. Chances are, the committee would have wandered for months (as many groups do), struggling to fulfill a vague, amorphous mission. If your committee experiences this, you actually have a splendid opportunity to exert your own leadership. You need to interrupt your work on the task and clarify your own charge, agree on the various sections noted above, and then invite your principal to review it with you.

Beyond this essential step of clarifying purpose and commitment, task committee members need to contract with one another just as self-initiating groups do—by becoming better acquainted, negotiating members' roles, and agreeing on ground rules that include your method of making decisions (see Chapter 4, pp. 64-67, and Chapter 6, pp. 98-100). For task committees, however, three special aspects of contracting deserve attention: discovering shared values and bringing up hidden agendas, identifying resources and constraints, and clarifying the relationship to the person or group who convened them.

Discovering Shared Values
and Bringing up Hidden Agendas

Contracting helps task groups discover both what they have in common and what divides them. Members of any new group come with an array of individual assumptions, expectations, values, loyalties, hopes, and goals. And because task committees typically are appointed, their members come with varying degrees of commitment. If members represent a grade level, a department, a demographic group, or an interest group, they will often feel obliged to act with external interests or constituents uppermost in mind. This situation is natural and inevitable, but at times it can seem as if an invisible network of forces, interests, and groups surrounds the actual members at the table. This becomes a problem for the group when these largely unspoken interests and attitudes *remain* unspoken.

We suggest that you start out by talking openly about what members share and how they are different. This allows you to be open about your capacity to contribute to the committee and your loyalties to others outside it. At this point, the central issue is safety: "How open and honest can I be in this group?" The question is best answered through demonstration, and the group might well begin with the positive topic of values. We understand "values" to be what people hold dear, the principles that are the source of your mission at work.

To discover the values you share as educators in general and as members of this committee, we suggest that each member share "what I value" statements with the group regarding the group's task. The question is "Why is being on this committee important to me?" or "What is it about the charge that appeals to me?" Unlike the self-initiating team, the appointed membership of a task committee probably does not share, initially at least, a passion for the project. By writing down the values you hold in common, you can create a short statement that can hold you together as a group if, later, you encounter conflict. These are also useful as criteria for the committee's later decision making; you can ask during the composing phase if the actions you are developing are fulfilling the promise encompassed in these common values.

Against this backdrop of commonalities, your group can now feel more secure about bringing up differences among members. Chances are that in your discussion about shared values, some of the differences among your individual purposes have become apparent. These may have been glossed over as the group concentrated on common-alities, and some differences may have remained hidden. Just like assumptions (see Chapter 3, pp. 47-48), hidden agendas need to be brought out into the light. They must be discussed so the group can be aware of them. If they remain hidden, they will inevitably become obstacles to consensus and trusting relationships. Even worse, they will be invisible so the group will have great difficulty even identifying them as obstacles. This seems to be what has happened at Sedomak Junior High, as Geneva's and Lonnie's concern about the school board's agenda has led them to view the group's work from an angle quite different from that of other members.

It is not always easy or comfortable to suggest that "our group" might harbor hidden agendas! One helpful technique is to place "Bring up hidden agendas" as an item on the first meeting agenda, or, if you are not the chair, to ask that the item be added to the agenda—and to the ground rules, too. This helps to legitimize a discussion about unspoken interests (other suggested activities can be found in Box 5.2).

However, some groups, especially those mired in a controversial or politically charged situation, may need a skilled outsider's help in bringing up hidden agendas. For instance, a consultant might interview committee members individually or distribute a questionnaire and then bring back the results to the whole group in a more open discussion.

**Box 5.2
Bringing up Hidden Agendas:
Suggestions for Leaders**

1. Raise the issue as legitimate and important to discuss. Establish a nonjudgmental approach, based on a spirit of mutual respect and acceptance of different capacities and relationships.

2. Point out that members are more likely to meet their needs and interests if the group knows what they are, and that with a full picture the group will function more effectively.

3. Review the techniques of straight talk (Box 1.4, p. 17), especially the importance of speaking for oneself.

4. Make it a group exercise: Ask each member to share interests, constraints, and external obligations the group needs to know about.

5. Model openness yourself: Identify your own loyalties and interests first.

Identifying Resources and Constraints

Once shared values and individual differences have been broached in light of the committee's task, the group needs to assess the practicalities of its charge as presented by the convener, whether the principal, the school board, the superintendent, or the faculty. As we have noted, the charge should indicate deadlines, the scope of the task, and perhaps what resources are available to support the committee. But the committee must make its own evaluation of these matters. The question is "Can we accomplish this task, given the time, resources, and energy we have?"

Although you can only estimate an answer to this question at the outset, your discussion about these logistics will make you all aware of the real conditions that will influence your success. We are thinking here of meeting times, locations and materials, support staff assistance, opportunities to research your task, and access to information within the school. Most important, if the group determines that its assigned resources and deadlines are inadequate or unrealistic, these must be discussed with the convener, and alternatives must be arranged before the group moves on. To neglect these logistics early on is to risk discovering them, as Steve and Mario did, when the deadline is upon you.

Clarifying the Relationship to the Convener

Finally, we urge as a part of contracting that task committees establish an ongoing pattern of communication with the convener or convening authority. As the group buckles down to its work, unforeseen issues will arise. Many of these will tug the group away from its original task as it was understood in discussions with the convener. If the convener remains unaware of this shifting focus, the group's product, when it is delivered, is likely to conflict with the convener's expectations, and disappointment and misunderstanding will ensue. Just as Steve in our scenario is conferring with Mario about the committee's progress to keep Mario in the loop, you will need to schedule regular updates with your convener. These will be valuable times to communicate your progress and, most important, to renegotiate your charge and your deadlines if your progress has carried you, as it may, into uncharted territory.

As you can see, we regard the contracting phase of a task committee's work to be especially important. Because it must occur on two fronts—contracting with the convener and contracting within the group—it is a more complex process than in the pairs and groups we discussed earlier. We encourage you to raise within your own task committee questions about the matters we have discussed whenever they seem to you to be affecting your success as a group. In addition to agreement on ground rules (including a decision-making method), shared values need constant reemphasis, individual differences and agendas need regular reconsideration, logistical obstacles require steady vigilance, and channels to the convener must stay open and frequently used.

Composing

Typically, the administration or faculty charges a task group to develop a school-wide response to a problem. Thus the work of a task committee's composing phase often can be structured around a problem-solving process. The benefit of such a process is that it can offer a sequence of fairly discrete steps for the group to follow; but there is also a big drawback in that the group can focus so exclusively on the structured process (the task) that members lose awareness of their relationships—*how* the group itself

> **Box 5.3**
> **Problem-Solving Model**
>
> 1. Frame the issue.
> 2. Identify the underlying causes.
> 3. Collect information.
> 4. Consider options and their consequences.
> 5. Select the best solution.
> 6. Develop an action plan.

is functioning. As we have seen before, that lack of awareness always leads to difficulties in relationships and in the substantive work of the group.

Many different models for problem solving are available. We like the model in Box 5.3 for its relative simplicity and inclusion of the important steps, which we will discuss in turn.

1. Frame the issue. This crucial first step helps the group focus on the situation requiring action. The goal is to clarify the current situation by *identifying the issue* rather than what causes it or what its solutions might be. "The issue itself" is the aim. The group focuses on describing the specific aspects of the school that require improvement—for example, existing practices, patterns of student or staff behavior, or how a policy has become counterproductive. Avoid discussing solutions so you can create a shared understanding of the real issue and what is problematic about it. It helps to write down the issue definition for all to see. The New Standards Committee, for instance, might have stated its issue like this: "Teachers have no shared criteria for determining students' readiness for promotion." Alternatively, the committee could have said that "basic skills are no longer central in the curriculum." How the issue is framed largely determines what solutions come up later.

2. *Identify the underlying causes.* This step is often a fascinating analysis of what lies beneath and around a problem. Having framed the issue itself, the group turns to discovering its essential causes. We emphasize *essential causes*, distinguishing them from symptoms and intermediate causes. It is useful to brainstorm potential causes first, then to categorize everything that has come up (four to five categories are usually sufficient) and to search consciously for the "causes behind the causes."

One technique, the "Five Why's" (used widely in Total Quality Management processes), asks "Why?" up to five times in response to successive answers. After being pressed five times to uncover a deeper, more fundamental cause, a group develops a rich field of understanding. In Box 5.4, for instance, the group discovers that one essential cause of the issue it faces is the faculty's varied backgrounds and disciplines. That analysis will enlighten the group's thinking as it collects information and looks at alternative solutions.

3. *Collect information.* Up to this point, it is likely that the group has had all the knowledge it needs. Now, however, it must look outward. The first task is to learn what others' experience and research have to say about the problem; a second task is to involve others in the school who will ultimately be affected by the group's problem solving.

Typically, members volunteer to take on various aspects of the two tasks, with the understanding that they will report back to the full group at a certain time. Several members might agree to meet with small groups of other teachers about the issue, sharing the group's analysis of it and asking for other perspectives. If the school is large, the group might select a sample of teachers or develop a questionnaire. The aim here is both to highlight the issue for others and to enrich the committee's thinking as it prepares to develop alternatives. To avoid setting premature expectations among other teachers, try to keep these discussions tentative and exploratory; emphasize learning what stands out about this issue rather than what solutions need to be applied.

Other group members can scan the wider environment, including books

> **Box 5.4**
> **The 5 Why's: An Example**
>
> Let us say that the New Standards Committee has identified "no agreement about basic skill requirements" as a potential cause of the confusion about promotion standards. The technique might go like this:
>
> - Asked "Why?" a member might say, "Because we don't talk about them."
> - "Why?" "Because we tried about 8 years ago and didn't get anywhere."
> - "Why?" "Because it's really hard to decide and agree on what the requirements should be."
> - "Why?" "Because we have different perspectives on what's important."
> - "Why?" "Because we come from lots of different backgrounds and disciplines."

and articles, colleagues at other schools, and university professors. There are many paths to resources: browsing or formal literature searches at college and university libraries using electronic databases such as ERIC; teachers', principals', and superintendents' associations; newsgroups and discussion groups on the Internet; and your own network of friends and colleagues at all levels. For something as central to schooling as the basic skills requirements at Sedomak Junior High, more resources probably exist than a few people can manage. The trick is to scan quickly and to go into more depth as a few resources begin to stand out from the others.

After your research, distill the essence of what has been learned, and share these highlights with one another. If there are options or conflicting viewpoints, be sure to include them in summary reports. These reports are most helpful when they are concise and centered on vital facts and principles.

4. Consider options and their consequences. The task here is twofold, and it is important to keep the two parts separate: generating options, then evaluating them. We encourage you to use brainstorming for generating options, emphasizing that the number of ideas (including those that might sound "off the wall") is what is important here. Start the brainstorm by posing the question "What might resolve this issue?" Let your imagination fly! List everyone's ideas, and firmly discourage the tendency to judge their worth. The classic example of this has a committee member responding to a suggestion by saying, "We've tried that before, and it didn't work." It takes only a little of that kind of response to shut down creative thinking. Fortunately, good brainstorming can fend off that sort of exchange (see Box 4.6, p. 71, for the rules of brainstorming).

Winnowing your brainstormed list of options to a few plausible ideas is a tricky process. It is very easy for the committee or its leadership to do this too quickly. You might assume that you know already "what will fly and what will not." But we encourage you to take your list of options to your colleagues throughout the school for some initial reactions. By engaging them in considering the possibilities, you set a tone of inquiry and collegial dialogue and help those not on the committee to catch up to your thinking. Ask them in small groups to "help us assess these possibilities." You can take the opportunity to point out pros and cons of different options and probe into people's reactions, looking for ways to clarify the options. Be alert to new suggestions that can arise spontaneously in such forums. The idea is to strike a balance between informing and listening so that such sessions become learning—and ownership-building—discussions for everyone.

After these wider discussions, the committee itself needs to evaluate the options. Developing a set of evaluation criteria based on your committee's goal helps you consider the consequences of each alternative in the light of what the committee hopes to accomplish. "What is most promising?" and "What is possible, given what we know about our school?" are two central questions, and it is helpful to discuss them at length, not pushing too quickly toward a decision.

5. Select the best solution. This step represents the climax of the committee's work thus far and is a natural evolution of its thinking. Problem solving moves from divergent thinking, casting about for as many ideas and alternative solutions as possible in Step 4, to convergent thinking, funneling more and more toward the solution of choice.

In setting its ground rules, the group has probably decided the method of selection, usually voting or consensus, and it remains now to make the choice.

We encourage your use of the consensus method because of its emphasis on group cohesiveness; consensus honors individual contributions to decision making and avoids a sense of winners and losers (see Box 5.5 and, for more detail, Chapter 6, pp. 103-105).

Members can use any of several consensus-building techniques. Here are two options: Each member rates each alternative (e.g., assigns each a number on a scale of 1 to 10), and then everyone discusses the results, working toward a

---

Box 5.5
Building Consensus

Consensus seeks out the best thinking of a group and arrives at decisions that all group members can support (not always enthusiastically agree with). Although all the bedrock skills help build consensus, these are the essential skills:

- *Encouraging wide participation:* including everyone in discussions, ensuring that all are involved
- *Interviewing:* drawing others out, asking questions
- *Speaking out:* being aware of your own interests, stating them clearly, and fitting them with others' intentions
- *Summarizing* (perhaps the most useful skill for testing consensus): gathering the threads of the discussion and offering them back to the group for consideration

---

sense of the group; or, with the alternatives listed on a chalkboard, members select their best option by placing a mark next to it, and then the whole group considers the result. Either way, we encourage you to compare and discuss the results, thinking of them as indicators of the group's energy and not as firm decisions, as in a voting process. Testing for agreement, the group will know when consensus arrives; often someone simply needs to point it out.

6. Develop an action plan. Some level of action planning concludes the composing stage. Refer to Chapter 4, pp. 70-71, where we discuss this step, and bear in mind that the actions need to be as specific as possible and should include the names of those responsible and deadlines for completion.

This overview of the problem-solving process will help your group design its work on its task. It will not, however, help you monitor how you are working as a group. During composing, task committees must be especially vigilant about two difficulties that often crop up in members' interactions: losing awareness of group relationships and addressing conflicts among members.

The first difficulty is that members can focus so exclusively on the task that they lose awareness of the group spirit, forgetting the importance of relationships and how individuals are feeling. We have found that regular check-ins and occasional process interventions help with this problem. They emphasize the importance of staying aware of connections within the group, as demonstrated in members' feelings and attitudes. Asking "How are we each doing right now?" as a meeting opens or closes or just after a major decision allows everyone the chance to step back and take a wider view of the group's process. It helps to make these check-ins routine and to give them enough time so everyone feels welcome to address any matters that are affecting their participation in the group.

Likewise, each member can keep an eye out for others' participation levels. Noticing that another person is looking frustrated, a member might point that out and ask about it, thus inviting the person to raise an objection the group may need to hear. Although this sort of intervention relies especially on members who are attuned to the emotional tone of the group (see Part II, p. 59), ideally everyone feels responsible for the quality of the committee's relationships.

Attending to relationships can build and sustain the group's coherence amid conflict. Conflicts typically develop around differences in style, philosophy, and personal affiliation. Dealing with them takes more than mere technique; it is not a matter of applying a certain exercise in a crucial moment! We offer the following suggestions and encourage you to supplement them with further reading from the resources noted at the end of the chapter:

- Talk together about the stages of group development, acknowledging that conflict is normal and needs discussion (see Part II, "Groups: Some Essential Features," p. 58). Make your committee's growth, and the factors that nurture it, a topic for everyone to be aware of and a legitimate subject of discussion.
- Stick by your ground rules. Review them occasionally, and post them on the wall when you meet. When people forget them, call each other on the specific behavior that causes trouble, using your best feedback skills (see Chapter 1, pp. 17-18).

- From time to time, take the pulse of the group and the immediate environment. Raise questions about hidden agendas, pressures from others at school, and expectations that may be developing in and outside the committee. Continue to honor straight talk by asking, "Does anyone feel we are being divided by our differences? If so, how?"
- If a member feels that divisions are growing, give feedback and invite discussion—as neutrally and nonjudgmentally as possible—by describing the behaviors that seem divisive and inviting others to explain what is happening for them. The essential way to manage resistance is to *honor it,* actively supporting the resisters and giving the whole group the chance to deal with the real cause of the resistance. The real cause almost always represents a factor the group needs to consider.

Attending to these and similar approaches to the committee will help increase its cohesiveness and may well spell the difference between a problem-solving process that concludes with loose ends and spotty commitments and one that receives the full support of the committee.

Following Through

With care and some luck, the committee has finished its composing phase intact and committed to its problem-solving plan. The committee's responsibility for following through will have been determined at the convening and contracting stages. The action plan developed during the composing stage should spell out the committee's projected activities, both for itself and for others.

We cannot explore the many following-through scenarios that might present themselves to task committees. But three key dynamics bear mentioning here because they often spell the success or failure of a task committee experience. The first is the "handing off" of the committee's work to the convener. This task will be accomplished best if the convener—the principal, the faculty at large, or whoever—has stayed in constant touch with the committee throughout the composing phase. In that case, the follow-through will have few surprises. The conveners will already have a good idea of the committee's product and the new roles and activities it holds for them. The most effective follow-through grows naturally from continual communication with the conveners *during* the task committee's life.

The second important dynamic involves the relationship of the committee to those who are likely to be affected by the committee's work. In the Sedomak case, the school's faculty will have to implement the new achievement standards. In our discussion of the contracting and composing phases, we emphasized the importance of clarifying the committee's purposes and authority with the faculty (and other groups, such as parents and students, who might be affected by the committee's work) and of involving others in the committee's problem solving. The benefits of doing so become clear now, when political influences otherwise might block the committee's actions. We strongly recommend, at the point of following through, that the convener and the committee together implement a strategy for successfully communicating with others and involving them in the action plan. The key point here is that the task committee itself should not be the implementer of the plan; the convener or convening group must arrange for the implementation.

Finally, task groups usually have finite tasks, specified roles, and deadlines. As groups, in other words, they end. We believe that successful task committee experiences need to be celebrated and that the commitments that members live out with one another need to be acknowledged. A meal together or a reception makes a wonderful occasion to review and to celebrate the experience—both highs and lows—and to acknowledge the roles each person played. Formal recognition from the convener can be especially rewarding, as can articles in local newspapers and the like.

The central feature of task committee follow-through is reaching closure *both on the task assigned and as a group.* In our busy schools, task groups often lose their focus, their membership, and their common commitment along the way. As a result, they cannot reach closure on their task or their relationships. The experience of serving on a task committee can discourage educators from agreeing to work on such groups in the future. We hope this chapter has given you sufficient direction to reverse this all-too-common experience. Task committees, we believe, will succeed as they receive the care and nurturing they deserve.

Facilitating Conditions

Task committees in our schools carry with them the hopes of many people: faculty, administration, parents, even students. Often, they feel as if they are working upstream as they try to make some long-lasting impact on their school. Like any other work group, they require attention, encouragement, and direct assistance if they are to succeed at their contracted tasks. Among these, we recommend particular attention be given to

- The resources necessary to meet frequently enough so the committee can do its job well (including release time for longer meetings or meetings at times other than after a full day of teaching)
- Information and consultant assistance where necessary so that the problem-solving and planning activities of the committee are informed
- Freedom from political forces that might grow up in anticipation of the committee's products and that can divert important energies and undermine committee unity and commitment
- Continuing support from and linkage with the convening person or group so that the committee feels supported, is able to obtain necessary information and resources as its needs evolve, and remains confident that its work will lead to action
- Assistance from support staff where and when necessary; committee members usually have full-time jobs to start with, and secretarial help can ease their work
- Recognition both of the committee and of each member for the investments they have made to assist the school

Resources

The problem-solving process and the work of task groups fill many volumes. We have found the following works particularly useful.

The final chapter of Dimock's *Groups: Leadership and Group Development* (1987) provides a good starting place for further reading about task groups at work.

A short article entitled "A Guide to Problem Solving," by Elias and David (1983), covers the classic steps of problem solving, emphasizing ways to make it creative.

Roth's *Problem-Solving for Managers* (1985) offers an interesting historical perspective on problem solving and includes two chapters (10 and 11) on enhancing individual and group problem solving.

Fox's *Effective Group Problem Solving: How to Broaden Participation, Improve Decision Making, and Increase Commitment to Action* (1987) devotes seven chapters in Part 2 to "A Step-by-Step Guide to Group Problem Solving."

Two resources present the decision-making process in groups. Fisher and Ellis's *Small Group Decision-Making: Communication and the Group Process* (1990) provides the theoretical and practical basis for communication as a basis for group decisions, and Nutt's *Making Tough Decisions: Tactics for Improving Managerial Decision Making* (1989) offers an extensive treatment of problem solving as a central aspect of decision making (see especially Part 4, "Key Steps in Decision-Making," and Chapter 15, "Managing Decision-Making Groups," for descriptions of a variety of group processes).

Finally, for a look at the task force as a special kind of working group, see Hackman's *Groups That Work (and Those That Don't): Creating Conditions for Effective Teamwork* (1989). Part 2 focuses on task forces and includes helpful examples.

References

Dimock, H. G. (1987). *Groups: Leadership and group development.* San Diego: University Associates.

Elias, D., & David, P. (1983). A guide to problem solving. In L. D. Goodstein & J. W. Pfeiffer (Eds.), *The 1983 annual for facilitators, trainers, and consultants* (pp. 149-156). San Diego: University Associates.

Fisher, B. A., & Ellis, D. (1990). *Small group decision-making: Communication and the group process* (3rd ed.). New York: McGraw-Hill.

Fox, W. M. (1987). *Effective group problem solving: How to broaden participation, improve decision making, and increase commitment to action.* San Francisco: Jossey-Bass.

Hackman, J. R. (1989). *Groups that work (and those that don't): Creating conditions for effective teamwork.* San Francisco: Jossey-Bass.

Nutt, P. C. (1989). *Making tough decisions: Tactics for improving managerial decision making.* San Francisco: Jossey-Bass.

Roth, W. F. (1985). *Problem-solving for managers.* New York: Praeger.

6

Send It to the
Curriculum Committee!

The Standing Committee

To the best of Tori's knowledge, the Awards Committee had been around since the beginning of Charleston Elementary School. The committee met quarterly to plan an awards assembly for the students, faculty, and parents. It had eight members: one representative from each grade, the school counselor, and the principal. Tori was the "rep" from the fourth grade, and today, a cool November day, was the first meeting of the committee for the year.

She was worried about the meeting. Her three fourth-grade colleagues wanted her to suggest some changes in the upcoming Awards Assembly. Feeling that past awards tended to discourage some children, they wanted to begin recognizing students more for citizenship than for academic growth. Tori's problem stemmed from the fact that the other committee members were all at least 15-year veterans at Charleston and seemed comfortable with its traditions. In her fifth year, Tori did not exactly have a firm footing for suggesting a major shift in the committee's activities.

After Ted, the principal, called the meeting to order, Tori had planned to ask if she could "make a suggestion." Ted opened the meeting by reviewing their tasks for the afternoon: "You're all familiar with our procedures," he began and went on to summarize each teacher's responsibility to "bring to next week's meeting a list of the top performers in your grade." Ann, the sixth-grade rep, then jumped in with an elaborate plan for displaying samples of the work of each honored student at the next parent-teacher association meeting. Paula and Seth piggy-backed on Ann's idea, and before Tori could think how she might intercede to make the fourth-grade suggestion, the room was buzzing with ideas for the PTA reception. The committee members, it seemed, were so familiar with one another that they practically did not need to discuss the details of their work at all!

After 20 minutes of discussion, Ted asked if anybody else had anything to add. Tori, summoning up her courage, said, "Yes, I wanted to bring something up that the fourth-grade teachers would like to do. We'd like the awards to recognize students who have made the biggest strides in citizenship this quarter. We've been noticing that some young-sters every year never get awards, and we think it discourages them. So we'd like to begin something new so everyone can be recognized for something."

The room was silent for a few moments. Then Stella, the fifth-grade rep, spoke up: "I think that's a good idea, Tori. We've noticed kids who are not doing well academically withdrawing some. But deciding who should get these citizenship awards is very tricky. When we tried it 7 or 8 years ago, we got an awful lot of flak from some parents."

Several other committee members weighed in with comments similar to Stella's—not outright discouraging, but not wholly in support of a change. Then Ted had to take a phone call from the central office. By the time he returned, two teachers had to leave, so he simply reviewed the date and time for next week's meeting, and the committee adjourned. Tori left feeling frustrated and wondering what the purpose of the Awards Committee really was.

The Awards Committee at Charleston Elementary School is a standing committee that has performed a function in the school for so long that most people simply accept its routine activities as part of the wood-work. Such committees play important decision-making roles in every school, carrying out valuable functions in the school and, theoretically at least, ensuring widespread input into their tasks. But Tori's experi-ence highlights some risks associated with standing committees: Their work becomes so routine that the basic purposes become clouded; the membership becomes so permanent that new people and new ideas are unwelcome; the guidelines for meetings become so ingrained that the committee grows insensitive to members' feelings. In the worst cases, standing committees become the butt of cynical jokes among teachers because they "take up a lot of our time and never do anything."

The challenge we address in this chapter is a major one in many schools: how to keep standing committees vibrant so they make constructive contributions to the school and are meaningful collaborative experiences for their members.

Convening

Unlike self-initiating groups and task committees, standing committees often have neither a distinct convening moment nor a definitive end point. Purposes established in the past may reflect a need that has long since disappeared or, more likely, been displaced by a new need. These purposes may or may not be written in bylaws or school policies. Likewise, the rationale for standing committee membership can become buried in tradition. As a result, faculty, staff, parents, and students can find themselves appointed to committees for which they have no expertise or interest, and, conversely, appropriate appointees can be ignored. For both these reasons, *before a standing committee's annual start-up*, its chair or convener needs to plan carefully the transition from the previous year.

The first step is to revisit the committee's established purposes to ensure that all members of the school community—committee members and others alike—know what these are. In many instances, these purposes reflect ongoing institutional needs that have been assigned to committees: academic departments; cocurricular councils; and such things as scholarship awards, curriculum review, staff development, and fund-raising. Their function is often considered essential to the success of the school. Given the staff time and energy they require, standing committees should indeed be reserved for essential functions. If the basic purposes of standing committees in your school are not written down, we recommend that you develop written missions that can be revisited at the convening meeting each year and at other necessary points (see Chapter 5, pp. 79-80).

The next step is to revisit the committee's membership rules. In one school, for example, the sixth-grade team requires that all sixth-grade teachers and the counselor for Grade 6 be members. Others, like the Awards Committee in our scenario, have been composed of one rep from each grade, and tradition has dictated that he or she be the grade's senior member. We recommend that as chair or convener, you review these membership rules—written and unwritten—before the annual convening meeting of each standing committee, and before new members are assigned or invited to join. Ask the essential membership question: "Will the members appointed in this fashion bring willingness, commitment, and expertise to the committee's tasks?" If your answer is "No" or if you are unsure, reexamine who the members are and how they were obtained before moving on. If your members are not all willing and able to be full members for the year, you will be starting out the year with the deck stacked against you.

With this review of the committee's purpose and membership before the annual reconvening (in August or September), the initial meeting becomes an opportunity to focus the work of the committee and learn whether the members are broadly committed (and able to contribute) to this work. We suggest you treat the new school year as an occasion for changing membership and reshaping purpose so that you are starting up again with a renewed sense of direction and a motivated team of committee members.

Contracting

Although participation and continuity in decision making are the strengths that standing committees bring to schools, creativity and innovation are their special challenges. You can begin to meet those challenges by setting a climate of renewal in the first meeting of the new school year. Note especially the significance of new members. They are not "a couple of new people" in an established group because even one new member signifies that *the group itself is new.* You need to work through all the aspects of contracting: creating a specific shared mission, developing working relationships, and negotiating roles. If new members are not part of this recontracting, they are unlikely to participate fully in the short run or, possibly, ever.

Unlike Ted, who opens the Awards Committee meeting in our scenario by incorrectly assuming the group has formed and is ready to work, the chair of a standing committee can best approach the contracting tasks as a way to renew members' spirits and create a reorganized, revitalized team. You might organize the year's first meeting (or meetings) as a retreat, take more time than usual for it, and plan *not* to make any important task decisions at it. In what follows, we focus on the chair's preparation for the start-up meeting of a standing committee and walk through an agenda that will accomplish much of the recontracting work. (The contracting sections of Chapters 4 and 5 apply here as well, and reviewing those sections may be helpful before you proceed.)

From the start-up retreat, committee members need two things: alignment around clear, shared goals and a new or renewed feeling of commitment to accomplishing them. Focusing on those needs, the start-up meeting agenda seeks to *involve the members* in exploring past and present purposes and to *empower them* to take charge of their direction. We suggest a two-part agenda for the start-up retreat. Part 1 emphasizes the people in the room, Part 2 the committee's tasks for the year. We start with Part 1:

1. *Welcome and introductions.* As the first event, introductions should signal both that people are important here ("Let's hear more about you than just your name") and that you really can enjoy your time together! If you have time, include the activity "Who We Are" (see Box 4.1, p. 65).

2. *Review of mission statement.* By reviewing the mission statement, you can emphasize that everyone, not just the chair, has an important role. To illustrate the mission, returning members can talk about the committee's past successes, how things have worked, and the committee's importance to the faculty and/or students. Ask experienced members to showcase the mission "in action."

3. *Hopes and expectations.* Invite all the members to offer their own hopes and expectations and list them on newsprint. This is an important moment because everyone contributes. The expectation that everyone plays an important part begins to set in.

4. *Agreement on goals, testing for commitment.* With the list of hopes and expectations in view, ask the group to suggest some possible goals that would help you all fulfill your mission this year. Then work toward agreeing on a very short list of goals (perhaps

just one goal) that are comprehensive enough to guide your work through the year. Encourage all members to help frame each goal statement and to express any doubts about it they may harbor. Draw out a sense of commitment to each goal, and explore the reasons for any lack of commitment. Invite all members to talk about their individual commitment here at the outset and during the life of the committee.

5. *Agreement on procedures and ground rules.* This vital discussion should review existing roles in the group: who the leadership is, how leaders are chosen, what their responsibilities are, what others' responsibilities are, who will take minutes, and any other operational roles that have a permanent function for the committee. Encourage questions and suggestions about these roles, as they will help all members more clearly understand their own roles. Even if you have a list of past ground rules, it is important to agree on a revised set for the coming year—for guidelines about listening or a method of decision making (see "Short-Term Decision Making" below). You might use the sample list in Box 4.2, p. 66, as a starter, remembering that you need to develop your own ground rules. Once again, the participation of new members in this process is essential to their understanding of the norms and practices of the group. It will shape their future participation and commitment significantly.

Discussion of ground rules ends Part 1 of our sample retreat agenda, but, as with all well-functioning groups, any member should feel comfortable reopening this discussion whenever issues of "how we're working together" begin to interfere with "what we're trying to get done."

Part 2 of the start-up process deals with the year's tasks. It is designed as an opportunity to think creatively about possible ways to pursue the goals without any need to make immediate decisions. After reviewing the work of Part 1, members might work through the following agenda:

1. *Crystallizing the vision.* The work begins with the goals that the committee agreed to during Part 1. For each of the goals, the group will need to build a common vision of what they might accomplish. We have found the "Crystallizing the Vision" a quick and effective means of doing this (see Box 6.1).

2. *Possible directions for the future.* Against this backdrop of new ideas, the committee can develop broad strategies for accomplishing its goals for the year. The task is to identify three or four ways that the committee could work to realize the vision. Consider using nominal group process (see Box 6.2), a structured brainstorming process to generate strategies, and then narrow them to a manageable few. The technique encourages some quiet reflection, involves all group members equally, and should call up a variety of

> **Box 6.1**
> **Crystallizing the Vision**
>
> 1. Write the goal as you understand it on newsprint, and check that it captures an outcome the committee wants to accomplish this year.
> 2. Ask the group to imagine an ideal resolution to the issue the goal addresses: What would be happening? What would that look like? Who would be doing what to make it happen? Encourage imaginative thinking.
> 3. Have each member write his or her ideas on a piece of paper.
> 4. Use the nominal group process (see Box 6.2) to capture these individual visions in one group vision on newsprint.
> 5. Identify which parts of this vision members think the committee is most likely to make progress with during the coming year.

possible strategies and actions that members can mull over before the next meeting. It helps to record the results, transfer them to the minutes, and circulate them to everyone. They constitute a rich source of ideas for action that you can draw on throughout the year.

3. *Assessing the work thus far, setting the next agenda.* Finally, in the last 10 minutes, invite members to say briefly how the retreat has gone for them, what suggestions they have for how the next meeting should go, and what the agenda should include. Suggest your own agenda items. Closing in this way asks all members to be responsible for the committee.

The start-up process, whether structured in a 3-hour retreat or in two shorter meetings, allows the committee to manage many of the

---

Box 6.2
Nominal Group Process

1. Ask each group member to write down his or her three to five highest-priority ideas about the subject facing the group. No discussion!

2. Go around the group, asking each member to offer one idea (not duplicating what another member has said). Post each idea on newsprint, without discussion. Keep going around the circle until all ideas are posted.

3. Give everyone a chance to discuss the proposed ideas for clarification, elaboration, and combining similar issues. Do not eliminate any ideas, but consolidate the list if possible. Rewrite a few if necessary.

---

contracting tasks in a relatively short time. Perhaps most important for the standing committee, its members have had the chance to join as equal partners in a spirit of creativity and possibility. If the Awards Committee had reconvened and recontracted in this fashion, Tori and the wishes of the fourth-grade team might have been honored, and the committee's performance could well have improved the way Charleston celebrates its students' accomplishments.

Composing

Standing committee meetings are often dominated by decision-making tasks. Whether an awards committee that meets quarterly, a scholarship committee that meets annually, a department that meets monthly, or a grade-level team that meets weekly, the meeting time is devoted to handling matters that have welled up from the school in the time between meetings. Many of these are immediate problems that require a decision from the committee: Who shall receive the award for citizenship, and how shall we celebrate it? How will the scholarship fund be distributed among the applicants? What will the seventh-grade team do about seven children with excessive absenteeism? Some matters, however, will require long-range analysis and planning: Shall we revise the awards criteria to include citizenship? Should the history department institute competency testing? How can the team communicate more regularly with parents about reinforcing study habits at home? Our suggestions for the composing phase will distinguish between routine decision making and long-range planning activities.

Short-Term Decision Making

Three activities lie at the heart of the committee's short-term decision making: gathering good information, using an open problem-solving and decision-making process, and monitoring members' investment in the process and the team. First, standing committees cannot make informed decisions without timely, accurate information. Our rule of thumb here is that information is seldom gathered *at* meetings; rather, it must be gathered *before* meetings. The leadership of the committee needs to develop an agenda, circulate it, include essential information, and make specific requests that members gather and bring information essential to the decision-making process (e.g., lists of eligible students or articles about a new curriculum idea). Such preparation can ensure that you will use the meeting for decisions, not for beating around the bush because members are not informed enough to make a responsible decision.

Second, standing committees' routine composing work benefits from an open, well-oiled decision-making process. This process must be conscious; all members need to understand what it is and how they are to take part in it. Even if members end up disagreeing with a decision, if they know and accept the process by which it has been taken, they can respect and support it. For this reason, the steps by which the committee is going to explore a matter (problem solving) and then move to a decision (decision making) should be explicit.

Schmuck and Runkel (1985) described three modes of decision making: (a) decisions made by a single person or a minority, (b) decisions based on the ability of a majority to overrule a minority, and (c) decisions based on agreement and support of the total group. We think of these modes as *consultative, voting,* and *consensus.* If the committee's role is consultative, the leader or minority who will make the decision depends on an open discussion among committee members and will benefit from encouraging the group's best thinking. During your deliberations, stimulate critical thinking and questioning to hear all sides of the issue (see Box II.2, "Eight Skills for Successful Groups," p. 59).

If the committee will decide by some form of voting, each person's vote must be as fully informed as it can be by an airing of viewpoints and information. Note how the suggested "Ground Rules for Voting" (Box 6.3) emphasize members' needs to understand and be ready before decisions are made.

Box 6.3
Ground Rules for Voting

1. We will discuss the issue until members are informed enough to propose actions/solutions.
2. We will discuss proposals until all members feel ready to vote, and this will be signified by voice vote.
3. We will restate the proposal before the group, writing it down if any member requests it.
4. We will follow Robert's Rules for casting hand votes.
5. All members agree to support the decision both in their conversations and in their actions.

Finally, if the committee decides by consensus, it will need to share information and viewpoints extensively so that members have ample opportunity to formulate a group consensus to which each member can gravitate (see Box 6.4). Bear in mind also that one of the advantages of consensus is its flexibility; it allows for varying levels of agreement in the group. A consultant colleague, Kirby Edmonds of TFC Associates in Ithaca, New York, sets out the levels as follows:

- Everyone enthusiastically agrees with the decision.
- Everyone supports it as the most appropriate decision.
- Everyone can live with it.
- Not everyone agrees, but no one blocks it.

As with all other ground rules, your decision making procedures will probably need to be revisited and evaluated periodically throughout the year. We suggest that you consider two criteria when evaluating your decision making as a committee: (a) Did it yield an "actionable" decision? (b) Do all members trust the process and thus support the decision (whether they personally agree with it or not)? Straight talk about these criteria can help you maintain a decision-making process that is both efficient and inclusive.

The third major activity for standing committees is to pay special attention to how members are feeling about the committee and its work. This is a special need because standing committees can succumb so easily to habit and routine. The Charleston Elementary School's Awards Committee meeting, for example, seems to have been scripted ahead of time; the old-timers hardly feel the need to be present, we would guess. The effect of this on members, new and old, can be devastating: lack of excitement, low investment, a desire to "get it over with fast," even absenteeism.

To counteract this tendency of standing committees, we recommend that every meeting start and end with a check-in designed to encourage straight talk. An agenda that begins by inviting members to share how they are feeling about the day and the work of the committee gives each member a chance to let others know their state of mind and energy level. Other pressing matters can be put on hold simply by sharing them with the group, and agendas people bring with them to the meeting can be put out in the open early. Refreshments and a relaxed setting help, of course!

Similarly, if every meet-

Box 6.4
Ground Rules for Consensus

1. We will discuss the issue until all members can paraphrase it to show that they understand it.

2. We will discuss it until all members indicate that they believe all opinions and all important information about the issue have been shared.

3. Proposals for action/resolution have been put before the group in writing, and positions have been aired freely on each proposal.

4. From these, new proposals have been developed that offer common ground for differing positions.

5. Each member will be able to state:
   - I believe I understand your position.
   - I believe that you understand my position.

6. All members will agree to support one position and to help put it into effect for a prescribed period of time, at which point its effectiveness will be evaluated.

SOURCE: Adapted from Wynn and Guditus (1984, p. 43).

---

ing ends with a brief feedback discussion, members have the opportunity—and the responsibility—to share the ways they felt successful (and not so successful) as a member of the group today. A straightforward method is to "whip" around the group inviting each person to note one instance "when I felt we were clicking" and one instance "when we seemed stalled." Following up with suggestions for "how we'll do things next time" can focus everyone on their responsibility to make the committee a lively and effective experience each time it meets.

Long-Term Thinking

Turning to your standing committee's long-term agendas, we have a few simple suggestions. First, protect these agendas from being squeezed out by short-term decisions! Often standing committee meetings are consumed by the business at hand. As a result, they must fight to commit time and energy to more creative—and perhaps more significant—tasks. Reserve a permanent place on your agenda for those improvement strategies you brainstormed in your start-up retreat. If it helps, you might ask a member to monitor this long-range planning task.

Then, to succeed at these longer range tasks, we recommend that you think of yourselves as either a self-initiating group (if the task is self-assigned) or as a task committee (if it has been assigned to you). For the portion of your agenda that is devoted to planning, we urge you to shift your entire mind-set as a group. Chapters 4 and 5 will come in handy in this respect. As you make a transition from decision making about the routine tasks of the committee to more actively exploring and creating, you will be expanding your repertoire of composing activities.

Occasionally, standing committees benefit from devoting whole meetings or extended retreats to these other kinds of work. For example, if the Awards Committee were to pursue a goal of expanding the types of performance it would recognize to include citizenship, it would benefit from collecting neighboring schools' awards criteria and spending 2 or 3 hours deliberating about what would work well at Charleston. Often, these experiences prove seminal in two ways: New and more useful ways of serving the school emerge, and, at the same time, committee members renew their excitement for their work and their bonds to one another.

Following Through

Standing committees have a special relationship to the school; they have been established to perform a regular and necessary function. The school community, then, expects something from the committee: a terrific awards presentation from the Awards Committee; an up-to-date integrated curriculum from the department chairs; a well-functioning safety net of programs for at-risk kids from the Positive Action

Committee. The committee's effectiveness hinges on its ability to carry its decisions into action in the following-through phase.

The committee's decision-making procedures need to include follow-through steps. At the simplest level, you will need to designate people to carry forward your decisions. Each decision reached by the committee should be followed by action planning; this need not be lengthy, but it must address the "Essential W's": What will be done? By whom? When? To avoid confusion, review the committee's work at the end of each meeting and restate each decision, the next steps, and the person or people responsible for carrying it forward. Record this information so that when the minutes are circulated a few days after the meeting, members can be reminded of their commitments. Be sure, as well, to communicate your decision and action plans to all people who will be affected by it or need to know about it.

A less discrete form of following through involves members in monitoring the school environment, seeking information on those aspects of it in which the committee has a special interest. The in-service committee, for example, ought to be attuned to staff needs that might become the focus of future professional development, just as it might look for evidence that past in-service activities have taken hold. Your membership on the committee gives you responsibility for the school's functioning in some regard, so you will all need to remind each other to monitor how the school is functioning in that regard *between* meetings. At Charleston Elementary, Tori has engaged her fourth-grade teammates in discussion about awards, with the result that they have proposed a new and, to them, improved approach to recognizing student performance. The information and ideas you bring to each meeting can only be enriched by such discussions.

We close this brief discussion about following through by pointing out the particular responsibility of the committee leadership. Clearly, the committee chair's or cochairs' activities between meetings significantly affect the committee's success. Standing committee members are busy people. They will need reminders of their follow-through assignments, just as they will need agendas and information before meetings so they can come prepared to participate. The chairs often carry decisions to other people, consult with members and others about upcoming agendas, and structure the agenda so the meeting will go well. These responsibilities, we think, require that chairs be selected with care and rewarded for the unusual demands on their time. Above all, standing committee chairs must be willing *and* able to exercise leadership both within the committee and in the school and community as they carry forth the work of the committee.

Facilitating Conditions

The greatest liability of a standing committee is that it is taken for granted, both by the faculty and by its members. If such committees are to play a vital function in your school, they must be kept vital themselves. We recommend monitoring seven conditions that will influence the effectiveness of your standing committees:

1. Give them the time and distance from their decision-making tasks to "reconvene" at the start of every year and to evaluate their work at the end of each year.
2. Facilitate the flow of new and different ideas to the committee throughout the year, making it clear that school leaders value its work.
3. Maintain regular communication among the chairpersons of standing committees and the principal. These people constitute an important leadership core for the school.
4. Maintain regular communication with the faculty to keep everyone informed of matters about which the standing committee is making decisions.
5. Rotate the membership of standing committees so that all staff have the opportunity to learn about and participate in the important functions your committees serve.
6. Periodically evaluate the need for your standing committees, and do not be afraid to alter a committee's mission (or disband it) if its function has changed or ended.
7. Recognize and celebrate the work of the committee, its individual members, and its leadership.

Resources

Two books directly address school committees' techniques for helping them come to effective decisions: Wynn and Guditus's *Team*

Management: Leadership by Consensus (1984) and Schmuck and Runkel's very helpful *Handbook of Organization Development in Schools* (1985).

Two other books offer advice on building participation and commitment in the committee decision process: Patton, Giffin, and Patton's *Decision-Making Group Interaction* (1989) is a down-to-earth "how-to" treatment, and Rees's *How to Lead Work Teams: Facilitation Skills* (1991) focuses more on leadership roles.

A short, practical guide to planning and leading meetings is Schindler-Rainman and Lippitt's *Taking Your Meetings out of the Doldrums* (1975). See also Doyle and Straus's *How to Make Meetings Work* (1977). For a book focusing on board and committee decision-making, see Tropman's *Effective Meetings: Improving Group Decision-Making* (1980).

Useful articles on meeting management are Nicoll's "Meeting Management" (1981) and Milstein's "Toward More Effective Meetings" (1983).

References

Doyle, M., & Straus, D. (1977). *How to make meetings work.* Chicago: Playboy.

Milstein, M. M. (1983). Toward more effective meetings. In L. D. Goodstein & J. W. Pfeiffer (Eds.), *The 1983 annual for facilitators, trainers and consultants* (pp. 145-148). San Diego: University Associates.

Nicoll, D. R. (1981). Meeting management. In J. E. Jones & J. W. Pfeiffer (Eds.), *The 1981 annual handbook for group facilitators* (pp. 183-187). San Diego: University Associates.

Patton, B., Giffin, K., & Patton, E. (1989). *Decision-making group interaction.* New York: Harper & Row.

Rees, F. (1991). *How to lead work teams: Facilitation skills.* San Diego: Pfeiffer.

Schindler-Rainman, E., & Lippitt, R. (1975). *Taking your meetings out of the doldrums.* San Diego: University Associates.

Schmuck, R., & Runkel, W. (1985). *Handbook of organization development in schools.* Prospect Heights, IL: Waveland.

Tropman, J. E. (1980). *Effective meetings: Improving group decision-making.* Beverly Hills, CA: Sage.

Wynn, R., & Guditus, C. (1984). *Team management: Leadership by consensus.* Columbus, OH: Charles Merrill.

7

Let's Team Up!

The Teaching Team

The remnants of a busy day lay all around them: open looseleaf notebooks, stacks of student papers, butcher paper diagrams drawn by kids depicting three "ancient civilizations," and the ubiquitous coffee cups, Diet Pepsi cans, and snacks. This was Team Alpha's weekly 3-hour planning session. Team Alpha, one of five cross-grade teams at Stockdale Middle School, included seven teachers who provided "core" learning to 150 students in Grades 6 and 7. Their mission was to integrate science, math, social studies, foreign language, and English in daily 4-hour blocks.

"That's a super idea, Paula," Mark was saying. "If we make our next 3-week unit focus on scientific innovations, we can begin with the Middle Ages, then pick up some major scientific breakthroughs in the Renaissance, and keep our chronological sequence going."

"Yeah, and the science of that period is so basic to modern science that it'll give the kids a good background for later in the year," Paula added.

Mandy, who taught art and French, added, "And we can show how the scientific innovations changed the way artists painted! So, y'all, when do we sit down and plan this out? It's almost 4 o'clock, and we're going to need to start this the week after next."

Silence momentarily fell over the group as the ugly specter of planning time once again arose. In its first year as a team, Alpha had planned its first 10 weeks in detail during the summer. But during the fall, the press of daily needs had overpowered the team's desire to continue planning, and now in November they had to play catch-up.

Celene, the team leader, broke the silence. "I don't see how we can do justice to a new unit like this unless we can get at least a half-day. I can go back to Barbara [the principal] to try to arrange that, but you know the problem we had with subs the last time."

"She's sympathetic," Paula added, "I know she is. But the district office doesn't seem to understand how the middle-level philosophy and the teaming we're doing require all this extra planning and communicating."

"You've got that right, Paula," Celene said. "I'm also concerned about the kids who don't seem to be able to do the independent work we're giving them during Project Time. This afternoon in Ted's and my area, we had a half-dozen kids who couldn't stay focused and made a mess of things for everyone."

"I know what you mean," Mandy added. "We've got about 20 kids, mostly sixth graders, who are still having trouble with the lack of structure. They're too used to worksheets and rows, I think."

Mark jumped in with "I know that's an issue, but we've only got another week to go on Ancient Civilizations. We've got to get something planned!"

"But we've got these kids in class tomorrow, Mark!" Celene said. "Ted and I—and all of us—have to come up with some strategy for keeping these kids focused, no matter what the unit is about."

"Yeah, I see what you mean," Mark added. "We probably need that extra planning time right away so we can do both of these things."

This brief glimpse at an interdisciplinary team meeting introduces an increasingly popular form of collaboration in schools, the working team. These seven teachers have come together, not to take on a specified task, but to carry out a complex function through an entirely new working relationship. Inspired by innovations in the corporate world, working teams in schools are a way of unleashing the creativity of teachers to tackle increasingly complex curriculum and teaching challenges. Teams aim to support better learning through creative teaching and reduced isolation among teachers.

Working teams in schools share several typical characteristics:

- They are responsible for an entire educational function (just as Team Alpha teaches all sixth and seventh graders), not just one task or specialized process.
- They are relatively autonomous and fully responsible for the work—including design, implementation, and evaluation—without intermediate approval by others.
- They often focus on one set of students to integrate teaching, subject matter, and services.
- They are established to be long-lasting, perhaps permanent arrangements for doing the essential work of schools.
- In composing and following-through phases, they focus simultaneously on collaborative performance, reflection, and planning.
- They most often range in size from four to eight members.

Sharing many features with other kinds of groups, the working team also has distinctive needs and opportunities. Team members work together more closely and more continuously than members of other groups, and so to a unique degree a team's success depends on the quality of its members' relationships. Though the differences between teams and other groups are mostly of degree, the phases of team development require some special considerations.

Convening

In some respects, a working team's convening phase is like that of other groups. Like a self-initiating group, for instance, a working team coalesces around a shared understanding of a need and a commitment to address the need together. Like a task group or standing committee, a team must develop a common language for its mission and values—both to ensure its own coherence as a team of teachers working with a set of students and to explain its educational philosophy and strategy to parents, other teachers, and the board. (Reviewing Chapters 4 through 6 can be helpful in these respects.) But a working team's membership issues are more complex (and are felt more intensely) than those of other groups, and these issues need extra time and energy.

Eventually, as we will show, the convening and contracting phases overlap for teams because the long convening phase involves potential members in contracting issues. Convening a team requires special consideration of three issues: timing, membership, and skills.

Timing

Whereas a standing committee convenes in the spring to begin its composing phase in the fall, a team—under the best circumstances, at least—needs to convene even earlier in the prior year. We suggest that convening begin in November or December and then extend slowly over the next several months until, say, the end of March. (Our calendar may require adjustment to fit your needs.) In our ideal situation, a team has an extended period in which potential members can become better acquainted, discuss the team's mission, tentatively explore what membership will mean for individuals, and begin to imagine what the classroom in a team setting would look like. Learning about one another and exploring one's own commitment are the heart of this phase. This is the time for visiting one another's classes to discover the range of skills and styles among you and learn the differences and commonalities that will become critically important once the team forms.

Mission and Membership

A team's success requires that each member authentically chooses to join it. As team members explore their possible mission together, they need also to test their commitment to one another. We suggest openly acknowledging the "trial" aspect of your convening activities. This way, people are apt to give the team approach an honest effort, and if they join the team, they do so with commitment, not because they feel forced. Agree early that the team will take time to allow each person to move toward the decision: "Do I want to be involved? Is this mission mine? Is this a good group for me? Am I good for the others?"

Convening can happen like this: One or two teachers and the principal, let us say, take responsibility for scheduling exploratory meetings with rather loose agendas and at various times in the school week, inviting teachers and other staff who might like to consider joining the team or who are just curious. The agenda includes talking about the team's mission and asking people to identify their values and discover those they share. Statements and lists develop, all marked "Draft." Participants directly address the questions of involvement, mission, and mutual "fit" noted above. Over the first several weeks, people come and go; a few attend more frequently, and by January or February a core group begins to develop around an increasingly clearer mission, a sense of shared values and approaches to next year's work, and a growing ease and familiarity with one another.

Before the team is fully convened, however, new members may need to be recruited. The danger here is that for the reasons just described, your team can form prematurely and ignore important aspects of membership. We urge teams, like other groups, to be direct and forthright about their composition and to seek women and men with diverse backgrounds. A reasonable goal is to represent, without becoming compulsive or arbitrary, the cultural backgrounds of your community and the students and to model cross-cultural and cross-gender participation. Almost certainly, reaching out to new members will be easier now than later.

Skills

A team must also examine its array of skills. A special requirement for teams, often unnecessary for other groups, is "multiskilling"—the need for overlapping or identical skills among some members (Wellins, Byham, & Wilson, 1991). In the composing phase, to ensure that the team's work goes smoothly, various members will need to perform similar tasks at the same time or substitute for one another occasionally. Five of Alpha's seven teachers, for instance, need to be experienced classroom managers and teachers because the team functions in five separate spaces, but perhaps only two members need to be particularly good writers. Now is the time to determine whether the team has adequate overlapping skills and to identify any new members who may be needed.

We have already hinted at the need for a wide range of skills on your working team. Besides the "bedrock skills" described in Chapter 1 and the subject matter knowledge required, the team might need skills and expertise in curriculum design, lesson planning, managing large and small student groups, presenting, tutoring, advising, writing, research, observation, and evaluation. Be sure the team takes the time to foresee its own actions (see "Composing" below), to identify the required knowledge and skills, and to recruit members to fill in any voids.

The convening phase often concludes with an intriguing sense of ambiguity. You recognize first the uncertain future, with the feeling of a long journey just beginning for your untested team. Just as important, however, is the necessary self-assurance involved in forming a team—the faith that "together we can do this, we can make it happen." The next phase, contracting, builds on and strengthens that faith, continuing to develop the team for its work.

Contracting

In our ideal chronology of the preparatory year, it is now March or April. Because the team has already developed its mission in the convening phase, the key question now is about relationships: "How will we work with one another?" Team contracting focuses on three areas: providing for leadership, preparing for team operations, and managing team members' differences in approaches and working styles. Although these issues will not be resolved fully until well into the composing phase, it is important to talk about them now, before the heavy action begins, so you can anticipate and head off major sources of tension once school begins.

Providing for Leadership

The use of working teams has helped to shift our ideas of leadership away from the image of the single leader whose primary, and permanent, task is to provide structure and give direction. The process of team development suggests a situational approach to leadership—that is, approaches to leadership based on an early need for direction and, as the team matures, an evolution toward the goal of *sharing authority*. Such an approach can help a team of educators manage themselves as a group of equals, without hierarchy or a cumbersome structure.

Kenneth H. Blanchard (1995) has developed a useful model called "Situational Leadership II," which describes four different leadership styles, each appropriate to a different stage of a team's development (see Box 7.1). At first, for instance, team members might choose a single leader who takes responsibility for leading meetings, representing the team to the principal and to leaders of other teams.

Increasingly, however, the team moves into alternative modes of self-management. Leadership roles can rotate among members, for example, or various members can take on different leadership tasks at the same time. In such ways, leadership grows organically out of your team's experience, and the team takes responsibility for itself, based on its knowledge of members' skills.

Although talking about one another's skills may feel uncomfortable at first, team members can talk about leadership more easily by thinking in terms of the team's needs and capacities. It may help also to use this part of our chapter as a springboard for discussion, helping team members assess the team's needs and individuals' abilities with a certain objectivity. If, for instance, the team is having difficulty sticking to an agenda, the most appropriate leader *for this phase* might be the member who seems most able to

> **Box 7.1**
> **Situational Leadership II**
>
> This model forms around four stages of group development (similar to our "phases") and suggests a different approach to leadership in each stage, based on the group's maturity:
>
> - Stage 1: An initial *directing* mode, providing a high degree of structure and supervision
> - Stage 2: A *coaching* mode, still providing structure and direction, but more actively involving members in the team's work
> - Stage 3: A *supporting* mode, involving a degree of shared leadership and reliance on team members' initiative and skills
> - Stage 4: A *delegating* mode, now that the team has grown increasingly self-directed and authority and leadership have become diffused among team members
>
> SOURCE: Adapted from Blanchard (1995).

intervene, calling the team back to the topic and keeping meetings on track. Agree about who will lead the team for a specific period, and schedule a review with the expectation that someone else will take the lead at that time. By raising the leadership question early in contracting, you can establish norms of straight talk, regular review and feedback, and self-direction and experimentation that will serve you well in the year-long phases of composing and following through.

Self-managing teams require a new relationship to the principal. The team's collective work and governance alter the principal's traditional patterns of decision making and supervision. To optimize the team's flexibility and responsibility for itself and its students, the principal needs to trust the team. We urge principals to think of their role as *supporting and facilitating* the development of the team, not controlling or directing it. By finding ways to support the team, the principal affirms a belief in its potential and ensures that it has the resources to manage itself. Needless to say, these roles require communication channels between team and principal that stay open and are used frequently.

Preparing for Team Operations

Two operational perspectives—long-term and short-term, strategic and tactical, both equally important to a team's success—often compete for the team's exclusive attention. While Team Alpha struggles belatedly to design the next curricular unit, it has to deal with the immediate problem of providing more structure for some students. The two perspectives are the warp and woof of the team's work; the goals and strategies run lengthwise into the future, while the day-to-day actions, the woof, shuttle across the warp. Both are crucial to the team's success, and it is important now to develop agreements about both the team's long-term direction and the ways team members will manage and carry out essential day-to-day activities once school begins.

A Vision for the Long Term

You can clarify the team's long-term direction by creating your team's strategic vision and goals. These are the kinds of questions you might ask (see Chapter 4, pp. 68-70, for detailed suggestions about visioning and goal setting):

- What do we truly want for the students in the long run?
- What do we want for ourselves as teachers?
- What aspects of our past practice do we want to keep and what new practices should we develop to make things different for our students?
- Where do we want to be next June?

Writing down the team's answers to these strategic questions will allow you to revisit periodically and perhaps adjust your long-term direction next year. Your vision for the future also sets the stage for the operational decisions still to come.

Daily Operations

How the team will manage from day to day is a greater challenge than the strategic vision. Your team faces two kinds of planning: policy decisions and operational procedures. Generally, the team will function within the school's established policies, and you will probably need to alter only a few policies that reflect your unique mission: for instance, communications with parents, an approach to grading, and management of discipline and absences.

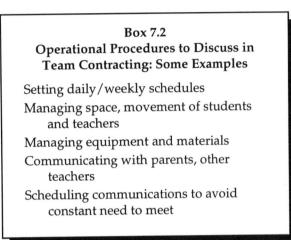

Box 7.2
Operational Procedures to Discuss in Team Contracting: Some Examples

Setting daily/weekly schedules

Managing space, movement of students and teachers

Managing equipment and materials

Communicating with parents, other teachers

Scheduling communications to avoid constant need to meet

After policies, day-to-day operational procedures (see Box 7.2) require a good deal of thought. It is important to anticipate how the team's school day will be different and to agree on operating guidelines that will help things run smoothly. The following procedural questions are analogous to those a task committee asks in its contracting phase (see Chapter 5, "Identifying Resources and Constraints," p. 84):

- How often will we need to meet?
- When will we schedule our daily planning, together and separately?
- How can we manage each day's schedule so that we stay in touch about how things are going?
- How do we ensure that we can each get help when we need it?
- Where do we keep the supplies, and how do we share them?

Answering such questions means imagining, in detail, the school day and week and thinking together about procedures that will help make things routine. (Box 7.3 suggests three levels of meetings that

begin to provide a proce-
dural framework.) The aims
are, once the new school year
begins, to provide an orderly
environment each member
can rely on, to avoid a constant state of crisis management, and to sustain a long-
term perspective in the midst
of all the action.

Box 7.3
Team Meetings: One Possibility

Consider this three-tiered meeting
framework:

1. Daily debriefings and planning for
   tomorrow: necessary for smooth
   operations and team coherence
2. Weekly sessions for assessing
   student progress and team
   strategies: crucial for keeping
   members on the same wavelength
   as they deal with students and
   each other
3. "Strategy review and team
   renewal" retreats, two or three
   times during the year, away from
   school, preferably with an
   overnight stay: critical for
   regaining perspective as the school
   year proceeds

Managing Team Members' Working Differences

Team contracting con-
cludes with agreements on
your "operating behaviors,"
the ground rules by which
you agree to work together.
The better you know and
trust each other now, the
more successful you will be
when the heavy weather moves in. Team relationships require a high
level of self-understanding, self-disclosure, and knowledge of other
members. These are essential elements of trust, the spirit that holds
the team together. In earlier contracting activities, many differences
among you have surfaced. Your ground rules for acknowledging and
capitalizing on those differences will be vital to your success as you
move into composing and following through (see Chapter 3, pp. 44-49,
for more detail about differences).

Fortunately, several tools are available to help team members identify and share their individual preferences about such things as work
styles, conflict management, and learning styles. We briefly discuss one
such instrument, the Myers-Briggs Type Indicator (MBTI) in Chapter
3 (pp. 45-46). In our Resources section at the end of this chapter, we note
several popular tools and places to contact. All are designed to offer new
ways of understanding how differences, if acknowledged and accepted,
can contribute positively to a team's performance.

Raising the possibility of using one of these tools with your team
members can feel like a daunting challenge. Others may be surprised

or wonder what problems exist that need "an instrument." If you think that one might be useful, we encourage you to bring it up with other members both positively and realistically: Describe it as an option that will help you get to know each other better for the purposes of your work. Avoid describing the instruments as tools that will fix problems or transform your relationships. Keep in mind that some instruments may seem unnecessary or too probing to some team members.

We have found that these tools help teams grow more cohesive and function better, but if members resist their use, talking about your different perceptions may be more effective than arguing the point. In other words, you may be able to open up, through discussion, the different needs of team members and still reach the same goal. Consider also asking a process consultant or mediator to help. The aim of the contracting phase, as we noted above, is to build understanding and trust, and if these are not created using one method, there are other ways to get there.

As the contracting phase closes, the team should have a fair degree of shared knowledge about itself (even if largely untested), and it needs now to agree on a few ground rules for staying healthy as a team. Because we have discussed ground rules for groups in previous chapters, two examples of different teams' working agreements will suffice (see Boxes 7.4 and 7.5). Note that despite their differences, both agreements emphasize the team's benefits over individual benefits and identify some important team skills.

Finally, it is important to end your contracting with a revisiting of team members' commitments. Each one needs the chance to ask again, "Am I fully committed to this team?" and to affirm, or not, his or her intention to move forward as a full member. If you have come this far, it is unlikely that anyone will answer "No." The long convening phase and the

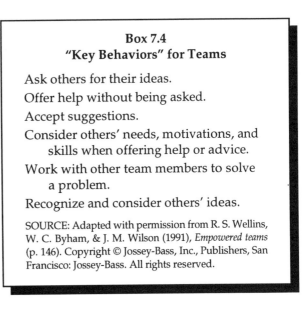

Box 7.4
"Key Behaviors" for Teams

Ask others for their ideas.

Offer help without being asked.

Accept suggestions.

Consider others' needs, motivations, and skills when offering help or advice.

Work with other team members to solve a problem.

Recognize and consider others' ideas.

SOURCE: Adapted with permission from R. S. Wellins, W. C. Byham, & J. M. Wilson (1991), *Empowered teams* (p. 146). Copyright © Jossey-Bass, Inc., Publishers, San Francisco: Jossey-Bass. All rights reserved.

Box 7.5
Team Ground Rules

Everybody commits to the full year; no quitting midstream over differences.

If any member asks for help, the rest of the team pitches in.

Any member may ask anyone else about his or her performance and responsibilities.

No complaining about another team member to a third member unless he or she has first been honest with the person in question.

SOURCE: Adapted from Wasley (1995, p. 58).

---

discussion of leadership, team operations, and members' differences will have provided the crucible for testing commitment. If everyone answers "Yes," the team moves forward, stronger and more confident, into the early stages of the composing phase.

Composing

The composing phase engages the working team in several activities simultaneously. In our ideal calendar, it begins around April and continues through the spring and summer and on into the new school year. Just as for self-initiating groups (see Chapter 4), the team's major activities for spring and summer include creating the equivalent of an action plan and identifying individual responsibilities for day-to-day activities once school begins. With the new school year, the team shifts into action. Unlike some other groups, however, the team's collaborative actions are simultaneous; team members are working side by side, with the same students and, in many cases, in the same room in a co-teaching arrangement.

The working team not only plans together, it acts together. In a sense, it merges its composing and follow-through phases by integrating its planning, action, reflection, and interpretations drawn from reflection. David Kolb's cycle of learning styles, presented as "The Learning Wheel" in *The Fifth Discipline Fieldbook* (Senge, Kleiner, Roberts, Ross, & Smith, 1994), describes the working team's activities nicely (see Box 7.6).

The team takes on these four distinct collaborative activities simultaneously and, to succeed, needs to build in ways to carry them out continuously. Here are some suggestions for making it work.

Joint Planning

Your team's preparatory work has provided a strong base of goals and strategies for working with children, relationships among team members, and ground rules to maintain them. Before school begins, the team also must plan specifically the teaching and learning you will carry out with students. This action plan incorporates the important elements of any plan: objectives, activities to reach them, designation of who will carry out those activities, time lines, and resources needed (see Chapter 4, pp. 70-71, for

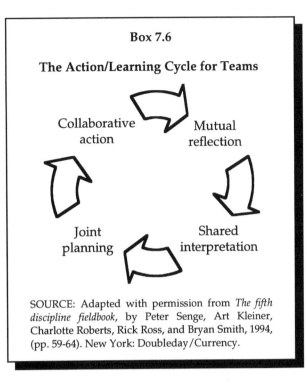

Box 7.6

The Action/Learning Cycle for Teams

Collaborative action

Mutual reflection

Joint planning

Shared interpretation

SOURCE: Adapted with permission from *The fifth discipline fieldbook*, by Peter Senge, Art Kleiner, Charlotte Roberts, Rick Ross, and Bryan Smith, 1994, (pp. 59-64). New York: Doubleday/Currency.

some detail on action planning). Once the school year begins, the team continues joint planning regularly, while you are taking joint action, as described below.

Collaborative Action

The rubber hits the road! Team members do their best to carry out their parts of the plan. This is often the most challenging phase because of the variety of activities teams can face: for instance, co-teaching a group of children in the same room; parallel teaching where team members execute the same lesson with separate groups of students; dividing responsibilities for simultaneous problem-solving conferences with a child, her parents, and a counselor; and consistently applying a behavior modification technique with designated students.

When you take action as a team, each member's understanding of the team plan and how it is to be executed becomes critical. The carefully planned lesson takes form, the conferences begin, or the strategy for disciplining Carl takes effect. It is vital to remember that at this crucial juncture in the team's work, things do not go precisely according to the plan in each person's head! *Differences in method, style, and personality* inevitably surface. Celene does not present a lesson exactly as Ted does, and Mark's approach to Carl is different from Mandy's. These differences will test your contract with one another as you strive to adjust, to maintain your unity as a team as you work with children and others. Much of that adjustment occurs in the mutual reflection time that follows collaborative action.

Mutual Reflection

The operative question when the team has finished its day is always "Well, how'd it go?" It is imperative to take time—whether daily, every couple of days, or minimally each week—to answer this question within the circle of all team members. Your "action" will rarely be as coordinated as your planning has pictured it, and you all may have different perceptions of how things have gone. So you need to talk about what did happen, why it happened that way, and whether it nonetheless may have fulfilled your objectives. This mutual reflection works best when every team member can report concisely his or her impressions of the day or week. Sometimes individual journal writing assists this process, as do various forms of check-in.

Shared Interpretation

Often ignored, this crucial step asks the team to forge a consensus on the important lessons it has learned from the action and reflection phases. Key questions for the team are "How do we interpret what happened?" and "What did we learn from this about what we need to do next?" You will need to avoid prolonged discussion about why things did or did not work and to be especially aware of members who might feel they have let the group down. It helps to write down on a flip chart for all to see the "lessons" each person draws from the mutual reflection, being careful to point these lessons forward to address possible next steps.

The Cycle Continues: Joint Planning

The time you have devoted to mutual reflection and creating shared understandings of "where we are with our students right now" has paid off insofar as it has pointed you toward some general next steps. Now, as a whole team, in pairs, or individually, you move to planning the next day's or week's collaborative action. It is often best to begin this as a whole group by structuring a team action agenda that includes these items:

- Major tasks and deadlines
- People who will plan them
- How and when the plans will be shared
- People who will carry them out

If the group splits up, as it often will, to do this planning, we recommend that it reconvene briefly before the next day or next week to ensure that everyone is on the same page.

We find the Action/Learning Cycle practical because it highlights the working team's capacity to adjust its actions, responding quickly and decisively to the constant flow of people and events. When you have internalized the cycle as a team, you will not need to meet formally to benefit from it. It can blend naturally into your team conversations, provided that your team feels enough trust and intimacy to support a comfortable flow of feedback to one another. Getting to that point is difficult because members are sharing observations about other members' performance—not just about what they think or say, but about what they are *doing*. When team members reach such a level, however, they shift into high performance.

A few brief examples can illustrate what we mean. One member thanks another for intervening with a child at just the right time, and for a moment both teachers share a reciprocal sense of having joined forces, without the need of speaking, to meet a common challenge. Or, in another instance, a teammate's suggestions come not as a criticism one needs to defend against but as a helpful correction to incorporate almost automatically into the flow of work. And then there are the extraordinary occasions when everything seems to flow more easily than one could have imagined, as if special effort were beside the point, and each team member contributes a needed element beyond anyone's ability to have planned. These are all examples of *synergy*—the spirit of a fully developed team, the sense that together we amount to more than our sum as individuals—and it comes from being fully present with one another, keeping the feedback channels open and sensitively maintained.

Following Through

As we have said, this phase is not so distinct for teams as it is for other groups because of the multifunctional nature of the team's work. As the team cycles through the Action/Learning process, taking action quickly follows on and leads back again to reflection and planning. Still, three issues about follow-through need to be kept in mind.

Expecting Problems

First, even with the team's developing maturity as the school year proceeds, it is helpful if all members maintain a certain state of readiness for whatever might emerge, suddenly or gradually, in the team's work. Expect crises and traumas, from the need for emergency planning that Team Alpha experienced to problems that students and parents will have as they struggle to adjust to the new approach, conflicts among team members, and misunderstandings and conflicts with others at school who, for a variety of reasons, may not support the team. We do not mean to be pessimistic about such things. In fact, the inevitable difficulties are "opportunities in disguise," openings for increasing the team's interdependence and level of trust. Expecting problems will keep the team ready to deal with whatever may come along.

Sustaining Straight Talk

A second concern in following through is how well team members carry out the actions that they have agreed to or that others expect of them—and how the team handles any lapses and disappointments. Problems of this kind usually stem from one of two causes. First, some aspect of the team's spring planning may have been incomplete or unspecific. Any vagueness in planning can lead to unspoken assumptions and expectations, and the chances are very good that one member's assumptions will differ from another's. Second, teams can develop an unhealthy habit of protecting each other from criticism in a vain effort not to hurt each other's feelings and thus may close up the communication channels. (Kruse and Louis, 1995, documented this among other team problems.)

The antidote to both problems is to be clear with one another about your expectations of each other and yourselves. If lapses in anyone's performance continue, refer to your ground rules (especially straight talk), and amend and strengthen them to meet challenges that emerge as the team develops. One way or another, it is critically important to discuss the irritants that otherwise can grow into major inflammations, let them fade away as they most often do once they are exposed, and then renegotiate members' expectations of each other. But if conflict has gone beyond the team's own ability to handle it, we urge you to obtain the help of an outside mediator or process consultant who can meet with individuals, pairs, and/or the entire team to expose and work through the issues (see Chapter 3, pp. 50-52, for similar concerns in a working pair).

Assessing and Celebrating Results

The intensity of working in teams and the constant press of short-term planning activities make it especially important for teams to step back from their work, assess their performance, and give special attention to celebrating successes. We urge you to schedule two or three retreats before the year begins for these purposes. Find a location outside your school and, if possible, give yourselves at least a day for each retreat. Design your retreats around two objectives:

- *Formative evaluation.* Bring grades, notes, and concerns about your students' performance. Discuss these, and use what you learn to shape your plans for curriculum and student management for the next period of time (see the Resources section for suggestions).
- *Documentation of successes.* As you take stock of the past period of time, highlight what has worked. Celebrate this, congratulating yourselves and helping one another see what you did as individuals and as a team to make it work. Build these practices into your future plans, and design ways to communicate these successes to your students, their parents, and the rest of the school and community.

The final retreat of your year should, if possible, last 2 or 3 days and come after students have concluded their year. You have traveled a long journey together and need to examine ongoing concerns and celebrate successes with regard to your work with children and the working relationships among you. We recommend conducting a systematic review of your curriculum and teaching practices over the year, targeting areas to redesign over the summer. Most important, reserve time during your retreat to review your ground rules and provide "straight talk" feedback on your performance as a team. This is the time for each individual to confirm her or his commitment to continuing with the team or to separate from the team for other assignments. Concluding the retreat with a meal that celebrates your hard work and your successes will close the year for you all with a sense of cohesiveness and satisfaction.

Facilitating Conditions

Among the many conditions that nurture team development in schools, these few are the most outstanding and constitute a minimal or starting list for consideration:

- Prior-year planning and development time (to the extent possible) for convening, contracting, and the early part of composing
- Daily time for reflection, sharing insights, and joint planning (the amount of time will depend on the degree of coordination the team needs)
- Administrative support, especially in the face of criticism from the public and colleagues that a team approach to teaching is too costly or (strange to say) "easier"
- Process consultation, training, and facilitation with an outside expert in team development (although the costs of these services may seem extraordinary, this kind of support usually saves the team time and energy and needs to be built into plans and budgets)
- At least a half-day monthly for assessment and planning
- Acknowledgment that teamwork is longer, more challenging, and more intense than teaching alone and thus that time and consulting support for two or three "strategy review and team renewal" retreats will be required

Resources

Teamwork and team building have been popular topics for education writers in recent years. The following are among the best resources we have found.

Barth's *Improving Schools From Within* (1990) is a superbly readable and inspiring little book for adults in schools. Maeroff's *Team Building for School Change: Equipping Teachers for New Roles* (1993), though short on the internal dynamics of teamwork, is a thoughtful discussion of the team as a key part of school structure and culture.

Kruse and Louis's *Teacher Teaming: Opportunities and Dilemmas* (1995) reports actual experiences with teams in schools.

Teamwork Models and Experience in Education, edited by Garner (1995), includes examples of school teams in action and emphasizes the need for cultural and administrative support.

Wasley's article "Straight Shooting" (1995) offers commonsense advice for open communication in school teams.

For a short book that has become a small classic on team building, see Dyer's *Team Building: Current Issues and New Alternatives* (1995). Part II is on "Alternative Team-Building Designs." Another useful book, with about 20 articles by different practitioners on a variety of team topics, is Reddy and Jamison's *Team Building: Blueprints for Productivity and Satisfaction* (1988). A chapter in this volume by Hanson and Lubin, "Team Building as Group Development," is especially useful for considering a consultant as part of the development process and includes a short questionnaire for assessing a team's performance.

Wellins, Byham, and Wilson's *Empowered Teams: Creating Self-Directed Work Groups That Improve Quality, Productivity, and Participation* (1991) focuses on the corporate workplace yet is particularly helpful in planning for teams as part of the organizational structure. A practical manual for groups and organizations of all sorts is *The Fifth Discipline Fieldbook: Strategies and Tools for Building a Learning Organization*, by Senge et al. (1994). Its application of Kolb's "learning wheel" is especially relevant to the topics we have dealt with in this chapter (see especially the sections titled "Mental Models" and "Team Learning"). For Kolb's original work, see Kolb's *Experiential Learning: Experience as the Source of Learning and Development* (1984).

A very practical resource that addresses schools directly and has been helpful with the Action/Learning Cycle is Herman, Morris, and Fitz-Gibbons's series of booklets entitled *Evaluator's Handbook* (1987).

The tools and instruments referred to in the section on contracting are available as follows:

- Myers-Briggs Type Indicator—Association for Psychological Type, 9140 Ward Parkway, Kansas City, MO 64114; 816 444-3500; also,

Center for Applications of Psychological Type, 2720 NW 6th Street, Gainesville, FL 32609; 800 777-2278.

- Personal Profile System—available from authorized independent distributors affiliated with the Carlson Learning Company, P.O. Box 59159, Minneapolis, MN 55459-8247; 800-777-9897.
- Human Dynamics Model—Human Dynamics International, 20304 Croydon Lane, Topanga, CA 90290; 310 455-1149.
- Thomas-Kilmann Conflict Mode Instrument—XICOM, Sterling Forest, Tuxedo, NY 10987; 800 759-4266.
- Learning-Style Inventory—McBer and Company, 137 Newbury Street, Boston, MA 02116; 617 437-7080.

In addition, annual publications starting in 1972, edited by J. William Pfeiffer et al., entitled *The Annual: Developing Human Resources* (San Diego: University Associates) offer a huge collection of articles, instruments, and structured activities for and about groups. An index, updated every few years, provides access to the series.

References

Barth, R. (1990). *Improving schools from within.* San Francisco: Jossey-Bass.

Blanchard, K. H. (1995). Situational leadership II. In R. Ritvo, A. H. Litwin, & L. Butler (Eds.), *Managing in the age of change* (pp. 14-33). New York: Irwin.

Dyer, W. G. (1995). *Team building: Current issues and new alternatives* (3rd ed.). Reading, MA: Addison-Wesley.

Garner, H. G. (Ed.). (1995). *Teamwork models and experience in education.* Boston: Allyn & Bacon.

Hanson, P. G., & Lubin, B. Team building as group development. In W. B. Reddy & K. Jamison (Eds.), *Team building: Blueprints for productivity and satisfaction* (pp. 76-87). San Diego: University Associates.

Herman, J., Morris, L., & Fitz-Gibbons, C. (1987). *Evaluator's handbook.* Thousand Oaks, CA: Sage.

Kolb, D. (1984). *Experiential learning: Experience as the source of learning and development.* Englewood Cliffs, NJ: Prentice Hall.

Kruse, S., & Louis, K. S. (1995). *Teacher teaming: Opportunities and dilemmas* (Brief to Principals, No. 11). Madison: University of Wisconsin, Center on Organization and Restructuring of Schools.

Maeroff, G. I. (1993). *Team building for school change: Equipping teachers for new roles.* New York: Teachers College Press.

Reddy, W. B., & Jamison, K. (Eds.). (1988). *Team building: Blueprints for productivity and satisfaction.* San Diego: University Associates.

Senge, P., Kleiner, A., Roberts, C., Ross, R. B., & Smith, B. J. (1994). *The fifth discipline fieldbook: Strategies and tools for building a learning organization.* New York: Doubleday.

Wasley, P. A. (1995). Straight shooting. *Educational Leadership, 42*(8), 56-59.

Wellins, R. S., Byham, W. C., & Wilson, J. M. (1991). *Empowered teams: Creating self-directed work groups that improve quality, productivity, and participation.* San Francisco: Jossey-Bass.

8

Revitalizing Faculty Meetings
The Whole Staff

We began this book with a scene we feel is almost universal in educators' experience. It is the faculty meeting at Sandford Elementary School. Wendy McClure, fed up with lengthy debate on homogeneous versus heterogeneous grouping, makes an impassioned plea to "settle this once and for all. Homogeneous grouping is the only practical way to go!" Sally Tannenbaum rejoins in an equally impassioned manner, concluding with "I'm sick of [teaching nothing but marginal kids], and I'm upset with the tone of this discussion!" Caught in the middle is Peg Stanley, the principal, who is trying to coax her faculty to a participatory decision about the school's grouping practices.

In this chapter, we invite you to think about your school's faculty as a group. For many, like those at Sandford, faculty meetings are minimally effective for working together. Too often, teachers, staff, and principals alike feel the way Sally did: "We study an idea for 4 months and get close to the end of the year and some of us push for a decision. And what happens? We don't make one. People always have too many objections or raise too many problems. . . ." The result is that faculty meetings in many American schools are not positive forums for decision making. The frustration and conflict they generate can even undercut the collaborative spirit throughout the faculty and the school year.

The faculty group is unique among working groups in several ways. First, the faculty is not a voluntary group; membership is a function of employment, not choice, and attendance at faculty meetings is often mandatory. Second, the faculty group is often large and heterogeneous; it can be unwieldy for some purposes, such as decision making. Third, faculty meetings are usually led by administrators; a hierarchical formality often shapes the relationships and behaviors among those present. And finally, many faculty members and administrators view the purpose of faculty meetings as coordinating those present; the tone of meetings is often tinged by parliamentary and policy-making rhetoric and process.

Clearly, these factors can block effective group process in faculty meetings, leaving teachers, staff, and principals frustrated. As we move through the four stages of working together, we point out the natural limitations on faculties when, functioning as "committees of the whole," they concentrate on problem solving and decision making (which can reinforce divisions and differences within the group). We encourage you to think broadly about the positive things the whole faculty can do when it assembles, and we suggest some functions that are more likely to build collaborative spirit and relationships than to erode them.

Convening

Of the two central convening tasks—determining mission and membership—the membership question requires less attention in the case of the faculty group. In most schools, the faculty comprises all professional staff members, and their presence at faculty meetings is expected. A significant question in this regard is often "Who else should be a member of this faculty group?" For reasons that will become clearer as the chapter progresses, we suggest that support staff be included in many of the faculty's activities.

The more consequential issue during convening is the question "Why are we meeting as a whole group?" Most faculty groups would offer two answers. First, faculties meet to coordinate their work and ensure high performance; they do this mostly by sharing information through announcements, presentations, and discussion. Second, especially in the current era, faculty meetings are viewed as an important vehicle for participatory decision making. The hope is that with everyone present, all sides of an issue can be aired, and a decision can be reached that everyone can carry out, even if each person does not wholly support it.

We suggest that faculty meetings can serve other purposes as well. We urge you to reconvene at the start of each year with a discussion of the faculty's function for the year (beyond information sharing and decision making). This conversation can revitalize the faculty group and spread ownership for its success. At the first faculty gathering of each year, put to the faculty the question "For what purposes should we be meeting as a whole this year?" Take enough time to engage every faculty and staff member in small-group brainstorming and priority setting. Generate your own best ideas for making your time as a whole group most productive this year.

As a starter, we suggest three purposes for faculty gatherings:

- *Community building.* The faculty can create a spirit and a culture among the adults of the school that will support open communication, willingness to collaborate, and optimism about your mission (see Barth, 1990; Sergiovanni, 1994).
- *Exploration of challenges and strategies.* The faculty can identify the challenges that members face in their work and create alternative strategies for meeting them that can then be developed further by smaller groups.
- *Decision making.* When the school as a whole requires unified collective action, the faculty can function as a committee-of-the-whole (for example, responding to a crisis or deciding a matter of educational policy).

Sharing this chapter with the faculty ahead of time and encouraging frank discussion of the limitations you face as a group can help make your initial reconvening discussion realistic. If you can arrive at a simple set of purposes such as the three listed above, you can build new meaning—and new relationships—within the entire group.

Contracting

The central tasks of contracting are to negotiate the faculty's purposes more explicitly and, in the process, to define each member's role and responsibilities in fulfilling them. Too often in school faculties, neither of these tasks is accomplished openly, leaving faculty members with mixed expectations about both. Some members, like Wendy and Sally, end up using the meeting to persuade colleagues to their view. Others may use it as a means to socialize or to feel connected to the institution as a whole. Still others may simply bide their time, participating little until the meeting (and their obligation to be there) has expired.

To clarify the goals of the faculty group, the leadership can build off the broad agreements about purpose from the convening phase: community building, exploring challenges and strategies, and decision making. Once these (and/or others) have been identified, faculty members need to contract with one another to function within each of these several purposes. The central point here is to be flexible. The purpose of faculty time together will not always be the same, and the roles and activities each person undertakes will need to change to fit the purpose.

Three specific points must be negotiated in this regard:

- Who will set the goals for each faculty meeting?
- How will the formats of the meeting be designed and led to match their goals?
- How will the group monitor its health and adjust accordingly?

Setting Goals

The first question is an issue of role: Who has the authority and responsibility for shaping the faculty meeting's goals? Traditionally, this has been the principal's bailiwick; increasingly, faculty committees or the faculty as a whole have shared the role. By emphasizing that faculty meetings can serve multiple purposes, we are encouraging you to consider a shared responsibility for setting the goals of each meeting. In your contracting talk early in the year, the whole faculty can develop a system for building the agenda for each meeting. In this process, consider the following:

- How often and on what days routine faculty meetings will occur, including staff development days if those are treated as whole-faculty events

- How soon before the meeting an agenda describing goals and activities needs to be developed, and by whom
- When that agenda (and any responsibilities to prepare for the meeting) must be in the hands of all faculty members

Designate a person or, better yet, a small committee to organize the agendas for your faculty meetings. Making this process explicit among faculty can give them a sense of ownership over the purposes and heighten engagement in both the planning and the follow-through.

Designing and Leading Meetings

The second contracting activity addresses the planning and management of each part of the agenda so that your goals are met. Meeting formats need to reflect changes in purpose and should be shared with the group before the meeting so everyone can come prepared. For example, initial exploration of the "grouping" challenge at Sandford calls for all members to bring to the meeting their own experiences and evaluations of grouping options, and the meeting needs to be structured so they can share and discuss them. On the other hand, a community-building activity designed to celebrate successes with hard-to-reach students might be structured as a "carousel," with 8 to 10 teachers exhibiting and the rest circulating among the exhibits (with refreshments served). Neither of these activities can be planned by the principal alone. Both require teachers to do some preparation so the meeting itself can be enriched.

During the contracting discussions at the faculty's first meeting or two, the group (perhaps in small groups) can brainstorm activities and meeting formats that suit each of the major purposes they have identified for faculty gatherings. Box 8.1 lists key considerations to keep in mind. Brainstorming this type of information for our three kinds of meeting pur-

> **Box 8.1**
> **Planning an Effective Meeting**
>
> Goal for this part of the meeting
> Information that members need
> Information that members need to bring
> Activities to maximize participation
> Closure or conclusion required
> Time, space, and other resources needed
> Leaders

poses can give all members the sense that they can shape their time together to suit their needs. The principal and planning committee can draw on these ideas to make meetings more varied, more participatory, and more worth attending for everyone.

Establishing Straight Talk

The third contracting task is to build within the faculty a capacity for straight talk (see Box 1.4, p. 17) about the usefulness of faculty meetings. Especially with groups that are difficult to convene and often ungainly in size and composition, a feedback loop is essential. Periodically through the year (and at least at the midyear and the end of the year), the faculty needs to assess whether its time together is meeting important needs. During the contracting discussion in the first meeting, establish a way for members to assess "how the meeting met your purposes and needs" (see Box 8.2).

The contracting discussion needs to clarify ground rules that will help every member feel responsible for the success of the meetings and the group. Ground rules can generate feedback about faculty meetings that is frank, constructive, and specific enough to be useful in planning and running the next meeting (see pp. 65-67). Commit these ground rules to paper so that all can refer to them and remind one another about them when needed. Often, if communication chan-

---

Box 8.2
Meeting Check

Stop the meeting 15 minutes before adjournment. Form mixed groups of five or six. Each group "whips" around its circle of members, asking each member to share straight talk about

1. *Purposes:* Did I feel they were clear, and did we stick to them well enough to achieve them?
2. *Participation:* Did I feel included, and was I able to participate when I needed to?
3. *Commitment:* Did this meeting build (rather than erode) my sense of commitment to our common purposes and efforts as a whole faculty?
4. *Leadership:* What suggestions can I make to the leaders of this meeting that will help them the next time?

Reconvene and discuss in a whole group, or share notes from each "whip" with the principal or planning group.

nels are open, faculty and staff will feel that the meeting is theirs, not just the administrators'.

Composing

Because faculty meetings need to serve multiple purposes, their composing activities need to vary to match each purpose. As each faculty gathering rolls around, you will need to recontract for each agenda and especially for each activity that requires faculty members to prepare for the meeting in some way. We share below some pointers for composing activities to meet each of the three major purposes of faculty gatherings noted above. In all three cases, the central task in composing activities is ensuring that a meeting is worth the time and effort the faculty will put into it. Time is often short. Faculty and staff have put other, often pressing, matters on hold while they attend the meeting. Your planning needs to maximize participation and a spirit of community despite the large size—and usually the afternoon fatigue—of the group.

Community Building

Faculty groups are often ideally suited to more open-ended activities designed to strengthen their sense of mission and unity. Faculty gatherings are one of a very few opportunities educators have to celebrate their work, share ideas and experiences with other committed educators, and rekindle a spirit of unified effort and a school identity. Community-building activities often do not require much time and can have an enormous impact on morale and on relationships. Think of this work in Scott Peck's (1987) terms (see p. 57) as "community making": the formation of a professional group in which all members feel safe, valued, and free to be themselves and to contribute to their school.

Formats for community building are as varied as your imagination. We suggest several types for you to consider.

Icebreakers

Begin each meeting with refreshments and a 5- to 15-minute activity designed to encourage each faculty member to share an experience, a feeling, a thought, or even a worry with one or two others. Prompts such as "Share one thing that worked well with a student today" or "Tell about one student you saw helping another this week" can build a sense of productivity in the whole group. Other more playful and personal prompts such as "Name three things about yourself that the others in your small group do not know" or "Share a brief story about your own experiences as a student" can break down walls among people and strengthen relationships. It is important to remember that icebreakers do not need to lead to any product or decision; their purpose is to build a climate of openness and a sense of community.

Celebrations

Take time to identify people and groups who have accomplished something or made a significant contribution to the school, sharing with the entire group some stories or details about those accomplishments and contributions. Honoring faculty and staff by taking time for them means a lot to the community, especially when those who are leading the activity are teachers and staff as well as principals. Celebrations that encourage all members to speak and participate often spread the sense of community through spontaneous expressions of appreciation, humor, and camaraderie.

Connections

Faculty meetings can build community simply by breaking down the isolation among teachers and staff members. Structuring activities that put weary teachers authentically in touch with receptive colleagues can be extraordinarily powerful. Techniques such as "Peer Consulting" (see Box 8.3) give each person an opportunity to articulate a professional or personal challenge with an audience of attentive listeners. Poster sessions such as the one described in Box 8.4 spur conversations and, in a relatively short time, give teachers practical ideas they can put to immediate use.

Whole-group activities that encourage the expression of worries, experiences with difficult children or parents, and even grief and anger should also be included here. In most faculties, a true sense of community comes from authentic human contact, no matter what the emotion or topic. Schools and their leaders can build community as much by facing conflict and disappointment within the group as by sharing moments of unanimity and joy. Our Resources section includes several sourcebooks for activities and processes for community building.

Exploring Challenges and Strategies

Your faculty as a group also needs to be productively involved in *strategic* issues— issues that are larger and more long-range than *operational* ones. Addressing strategic issues early often forestalls major crises and operational problems in the future. Faculty meetings are a prime opportunity to have everyone think about "the big picture" issues. As teachers, counselors, and support staff explore the challenges the school is facing or soon will face surrounding, say, growing numbers of latch-key kids or changing employment needs, they will be preparing themselves and the school to respond to these issues.

Strategic thinking needs to be nurtured and sustained over time. Designing composing activities in this regard requires leadership to structure parts of several faculty meetings to engage faculty with the challenge

---

Box 8.3
Peer Consulting

Four to six colleagues join together. Each person receives 15 minutes of "consulting" from his or her colleagues as follows:

1. One member describes in detail a problematic situation he or she faces (3 minutes).
2. Each of the other members, in turn, offers advice and counsel on how to address the situation (3 minutes each).
3. No discussion is required; when all are finished, another member offers a problematic situation.

If one colleague records notes for each presenter, each person goes away from the session with written ideas to consider.

Box 8.4
What Works for Me

Goal: Share practices that work and celebrate our accomplishments as a faculty

Information needed: Instructions for sharing at meeting

Information to bring: Prepare a visual depicting one success you had with some students this month

Participation: Everyone should have access to every success; hold poster session with coffee and cookies

Closure: Whole-group sharing of observations about what seems to be working for us

Logistics: Wall space, circulation space, 20 minutes

Leaders: English Dept.

Box 8.5
**Three Questions to Ask (to Identify a
Strategic Issue)**

1. What is the issue? Phrase it as a question that the school can take some action on (but don't worry about the action yet!).
2. Why is this an issue? What is it about the mission of our school and the situation we are responding to that makes this a strategic rather than operational matter (i.e., why must we involve our whole faculty over a period of time)?
3. What happens if we do *not* address this issue?

SOURCE: Adapted from Bryson (1988, pp. 159-160).

you have identified. It is helpful to start off with the whole faculty to "frame" the issue (see Box 8.5). Subsequent activities designed to "explore our challenges" with regard to the issue frequently work better in small groups facilitated by colleagues who can maintain the focus on strategic thinking. Finally, your faculty can generate possible strategies to meet the challenge you have identified, test out the practicality of these strategies, and eventually select one or several for use in your school (see Box 5.3, p. 85). The agenda for a meeting on the integration of non-English-speaking children (see Box 8.6) illustrates an activity designed to yield possible future strategies and to refer it to a subgroup for decision.

We cannot overstate the value of devoting faculty time to strategic thinking. Your school's faculty possesses the educational expertise and the professional responsibility to address long-range questions of curriculum, pedagogy, and student management. By devoting time to three or four major issues each year, your faculty will keep itself current and position itself to make informed and thoughtful decisions in response to changing conditions. Strategic thinking will not be left to the principal, the superintendent, or the school board alone. Thus your school need not play out that oft-repeated scenario in which the "administration comes down and tells us what we've got to do now."

Organizing for Decision Making

Faculties of up to about 15 members can usually function as a committee of the whole. They can meet frequently and operate fluidly, solving problems and arriving at decisions. They often function more as a standing committee (Chapter 6) or a working team (Chapter 7) than as a parliamentary body.

Faculties of more than 15 to 20 people, however, have more difficulty analyzing a problem, exploring alternative solutions, and arriving at a decision that all can smoothly execute. For this reason, we recommend that committees be assigned to do the more time-consuming research and analysis that must precede decisions. Structure your work and your people so that

1. The whole faculty typically does not generate a detailed plan, policy, or activity.

2. The whole faculty is often asked to identify

   a. General principles and goals for children that should guide a committee's work

   b. The committee's charge, including parameters within which the committee is to work (e.g., "What is the committee *not* to work on? What are the deadlines and real limits they should work within?")

   c. Whether and how they want to be involved in a final decision on the matter (or if the committee itself can follow through on its own)

3. When a committee is to report back to the whole faculty, it should supply ahead of time to each faculty member a synopsis

---

Box 8.6
Agenda Item: Integrating Non-English-Speaking Children

Goal: Evaluate progress on integrating non-English-speaking children socially into the school

Information needed: Questions to think about regarding your non-English-speaking students prior to meeting

Information to bring: Answers to these questions, in note form, with examples

Participation: In small, cross-grade groups of five; share observations from notes; identify common successes and challenges

Closure: Compile commonalities from groups on newsprint; brainstorm possible strategies to address most common challenges; refer to Team Leader Committee

Logistics: Circular tables for five (cafeteria); 1 hour; drinks and munchies

Leaders: Guidance director and ESL teacher

of the information it gathered, descriptions of alternative actions it considered, and a rationale for the alternative it is proposing.

Your objective is to use the whole faculty's time for decision making, not for lengthy information-sharing and solution-finding discussion. We have included in Box 8.7 a sample meeting plan for leading a decision-making activity. In this case, a committee has studied three alternative science curricula and has assessed their "pros and cons," listing them for the whole faculty in a written synopsis. The synopsis, along with this brief plan, has been distributed to everyone a week before the faculty meeting with a list of the committee members and an invitation to speak with any of them for more information before the faculty meeting. The expectation, then, is that everyone will be ready to make a decision at the meeting.

Box 8.7
Choosing a Science Curriculum

Goal: Choose one science curriculum from among the three we have studied

Information needed: Synopsis of the three with pros and cons

Information to bring: Assessment of each

Participation: Open discussion of each alternative, focusing on relative strengths; straw poll; further discussion; reach consensus

Closure: Consensus (no "absolutely not" members)

Logistics: Seating for everyone in a circle or amphitheater setup

Leaders: Principal and committee chairs

Faculties sometimes are called on to make crisis decisions. When a school has experienced a tragedy or faces an immediate challenge such as a community attack or budget cut, time often does not permit lengthy study or deliberation. In these instances, leaders must provide a way for every faculty member to be heard and to be a part of a decision or response. Use of small groups for sharing reactions and ideas and then bringing together their thoughts and feelings through public reporting or a nominal group process (see Box 6.2, p. 102) can generate excellent ideas while involving everyone. A small leadership team that both plans and facilitates the process can enhance whole-group decisions in such circumstances. Team members also can facilitate small-group meetings in emergencies without the logistical hassle of convening the whole group.

We hope these suggestions for composing have challenged you to think of your faculty meetings as arenas for thoughtfulness and comradeship as well as for decisions. Currently, faculty meetings are a major challenge for many schools because their purposes have been too narrow and their leadership has fallen to the principals alone. Faculty gatherings are prime opportunities to unify your school, weaving task groups, grade-level teams, departments, and all staff members into one professional community. By making your time together stimulating, productive, and enjoyable, you will create a vibrant culture.

Following Through

Just as faculty meetings will differ in their purposes, the follow-through will differ to suit the purpose. A basic point to remember is that at the end of each agenda item and perhaps reiterated at the end of the meeting, follow-through steps need to be publicly stated, preferably in writing, along with the designation of who will be responsible for them and by what deadline. Here are some reminders that can help.

Community Building

The intent of community-building activities is unabashedly to help everyone feel more like a team, to share an understanding of their purposes, and to empathize with and support all members in their own efforts to make the team succeed. We think of community-building follow-through as carrying forward beyond a meeting a sense that "I am working in a good school with good people," a spirit of "we-ness" that can encourage and sustain each person in the days and weeks ahead. More specifically, community building forms relationships that help teachers and staff ask for help from one another, offer help to one another, and solve problems together instead of in isolation.

For the faculty, then, following through shows most clearly in pairs or small groups. Conversations started in faculty meetings can lead in myriad directions: to a pair of teachers sharing materials, to a small-group meeting about a child, or to leaving an encouraging note in a colleague's mailbox. Community building gives value to each adult in the school; it nurtures open communication and collaboration. You can feel the benefits of positive collegial relationships in these activities, and these feelings in turn often stimulate new actions that directly help children.

Exploring Challenges and Strategies

Following through for these kinds of faculty activities is often difficult because "next steps" are not always self-evident in the process of studying an issue and exploring alternatives. We suggest that a small task group oversee the important activities that must occur between meetings if strategic exploration is to succeed. These committees can have a specified responsibility and a limited life. For example, the charge to such a committee could be: "The 'steering committee' for the faculty's study of integrating non-English-speaking students will (a) gather sample curriculum and procedures from other schools, (b) share these with the faculty, (c) develop curriculum suggestions and a procedure for our school, and (d) report these back to the whole faculty by February 1."

Strategic planning requires study, sharing of information, and extensive discussion among the faculty and staff. From this process, the faculty may discover that no new practices or policy decisions are needed. Even though follow-through into action may not be called for, the strategic-thinking process has educated everyone about the important issue and has left everyone ready to move to action should that be called for in the future. On the other hand, if the faculty's study leads to a consensus that "something needs to be done about this," then the group can follow through by moving to strategic planning, action planning, and a final decision (see Chapters 5 and 6). The administration and the "steering" or "study" committee then must negotiate specific steps and responsibilities with the whole faculty in much the same way as a task group would.

Decision Making

How many times have you participated in a lengthy faculty meeting, straining to make a consensus decision, only to have it die in the following-through phase? If the faculty as a whole has made a decision about a policy, a curriculum, or some other proposal, frequently the follow-through is left unspecified. We recommend that a person or small group be assigned to develop a plan for implementing each decision and for reporting back through memo or in person the expectations for each faculty and staff member to carry out the decision. The principal and teacher leadership can ensure coordination of these follow-through activities.

If the faculty has delegated decision making to a committee, the committee likewise has a follow-through responsibility to report back to the faculty. Again, the decision itself is usually not as important to people as is its implementation. A committee might report that it has designed a new intervention strategy for at-risk fourth graders. Merely being informed of that decision does not help each staff member know what his or her responsibilities are in making the intervention work for fourth graders! As with decisions made by the whole faculty, both the decision (with its rationale) and its operational steps need to be shared with everyone who is expected to carry it out.

The following-through phase significantly shapes your perception that "going to that faculty meeting was worthwhile." As you plan faculty gatherings, keep your eye on the outcomes for your colleagues and for students. Strive for follow-through that gives all members the sense that their participation in faculty meetings makes a difference to students, to them, and to the school as a whole. Most important, make sure that your convening, contracting, and composing activities help the faculty group focus its time and energies on outcomes they can follow through on.

Facilitating Conditions

The spaces and schedules of schools are not constructed with large gatherings of adults in mind. To facilitate the faculty's formation as a group and community, these conditions will be important to bear in mind:

- A space (outside your school, if need be) that can comfortably accommodate your faculty group and permit members to talk with one another as a whole group and/or in small groups
- A modest budget for refreshments and to fund information-gathering activities to support effective decision making and strategic planning
- A recorder/secretary so that important decisions and information are written down (a) publicly so the group can see and discuss them and (b) at the end of the meeting or after the

meeting so everyone has a summary of decisions, operational plans, and other useful information

- A widespread belief among faculty and staff members that they are a community of educators and that, as a community, they can benefit and grow from celebrating successes, confronting challenges, and growing professionally with one another

- Leaders in both the administration and faculty who are willing to make whole-faculty time the responsibility of all faculty and staff by sharing control over the purposes, agendas, leadership, and follow-through of meetings

Resources

We refer you to the Resources section of Chapter 6 for assistance in structuring and conducting meetings. In addition, the following have been useful in the more formal aspects of faculty meetings: Fletcher's *Meetings, Meetings* (1983) and Bradford's *Making Meetings Work: A Guide for Leaders and Group Members* (1976).

Particularly helpful in dealing with conflict or resistance in meetings are Chapter 9, "Managing Resistance," in *Interactions: Collaboration Skills for School Professionals*, by Friend and Cook (1992) and Marshall's *Handling Difficult Behavior at Meetings* (1984).

For ideas and strategies to use in building a sense of community within your faculty, an excellent resource for the entire faculty to read is Barth's *Improving Schools From Within* (1990). Helpful in addressing the dynamics of faculty functioning as a "community of leaders" are Chapters 7 and 8 from *Making Sense as a School Leader: Persisting Tensions, Creative Opportunities* by Ackerman, Donaldson, and van der Bogert (1996). Sergiovanni's *Building Community in Schools* (1994) presents an inspiring and convincing case with many examples from schools. Finally, several of the essays in Lieberman's edited volume *Building a Professional Culture in Schools* (1988) offer superb discussions of school-wide approaches to collaboration, including ideas for culture building (see especially McLaughlin and Yee's "School as a Place to Have a Career."

Two more general resources cited in this chapter are Peck's *The Different Drum: Community-Making and Peace* (1987) and Bryson's *Strategic Planning for Public and Nonprofit Organizations: A Guide to Strengthening and Sustaining Organizational Achievement* (1988).

References

Ackerman, R., Donaldson, G., & van der Bogert, R. (1996). *Making sense as a school leader: Persisting tensions, creative opportunities.* San Francisco: Jossey-Bass.

Barth, R. (1990). *Improving schools from within.* San Francisco: Jossey-Bass.

Bradford, L. (1976). *Making meetings work: A guide for leaders and group members.* San Diego: University Associates.

Bryson, J. (1988). *Strategic planning for public and nonprofit organizations: A guide to strengthening and sustaining organizational achievement.* San Francisco: Jossey-Bass.

Fletcher, W. (1983). *Meetings, meetings.* New York: William Morrow.

Friend, M., & Cook, L. (1992). *Interactions: Collaboration skills for school professionals.* New York: Longman.

Lieberman, A. (Ed.). (1988). *Building a professional culture in schools.* New York: Teachers College Press.

Marshall, J. (1984). *Handling difficult behavior at meetings.* Reston, VA: Marshall House.

McLaughlin, M., & Mei-ling Yee, S. (1988). School as a place to have a career. In A. Lieberman (Ed.), *Building a professional culture in schools* (pp. 23-44). New York: Teachers College Press.

Peck, M. S. (1987). *The different drum: Community-making and peace.* New York: Simon & Schuster.

Sergiovanni, T. (1994). *Building community in schools.* San Francisco: Jossey-Bass.

9

Collaboration

Making It Happen

To us, the biggest risk in education is not taking one.

—Seymour Sarason (1991, p. 176)

Our concluding chapter addresses the themes that make a central difference in the success of collaborative efforts. We emphasize that the most important factor in your success is the willingness of each person to commit to working together in an open, authentic manner. Our guidelines for developing working relationships and the bedrock skills they require should get you and your colleagues started well along this road. But other forces also influence the success and quality of collaboration.

The themes in this chapter stem from forces inside and outside yourself that can erode collaboration if you do not remain aware of them and act on them. The first of these is handling conflict and frustration; the second is addressing your need for supportive conditions within the school and district.

Handling Conflict and Frustration: Acknowledging Your Limits

Perhaps you have felt doubtful, even skeptical, at various points in our book. You may have thought, "That sounds good, but I can't see it working in my school" or "I can't imagine people being that honest with each other on my team." These are natural reactions stemming from an undeniable characteristic of collaborative work: it is often more challenging and more time consuming than working alone is. The rewards of collaboration include creative ways to work with your students and each other and a spirit of personal growth, professional excitement, and camaraderie. But at times such prizes seem mockingly elusive.

We have found that being clear about the frustrations that arise as we work together can take the edge off their sharpness and help us find ways to mitigate their power. For all of us, it is our own awareness that allows us to transform problems into opportunities. We see four common forms of frustration that educators feel when trying to collaborate (they have all been illustrated in the scenarios at the beginning of our chapters). We will briefly describe each one and suggest how it might be managed.

External Obstacles

Few educators need to be reminded how the school schedule, space, reward system, and hierarchy can thwart their efforts to work together. Indeed, these external obstacles present you with reasons *not* to collaborate. As each chapter's list of Facilitating Conditions implies, schools are not usually organized to support adult partnerships; rather, one teacher is assigned to teach one group of students on the assumption that his or her specialized knowledge and responsibility justify that assignment. These expectations for individual work are deeply embedded in our school structures, policies, and culture. You cannot expect them to vanish simply because you and some colleagues wish them to!

So how might you deal with the frustration arising from these obstacles? We have three suggestions:

1. Where possible, include your principal in the communication loop as you convene and contract. If the principal (as well as

other leaders within the school) knows that you are shifting your work patterns for the good of your students, he or she can be prepared to assist you when obstacles appear.

2. Work around the obstacles; do not take them on directly unless you are confident that you can remove them without disrupting your working together. Schools offer adults considerable freedom to form networks and working relationships on their own. Most external obstacles are so much a part of the system that you will have difficulty removing them altogether (indeed, the restructuring movement has attempted to do this, with unremarkable results).

3. Make your working relationship with your partner or in your group rewarding for you all. Start small and build a solid foundation. As you work together, your ability to effect change in the institution will grow. Obstacles that seemed overwhelming in the first year can appear smaller and more manageable in subsequent years.

Obstacles Within the Pair or Group

Frustrations that stem from your working relationships can also dampen your commitment to collaboration. Few working relationships come to fruition unless differences of opinion, style, and philosophy have surfaced at some point. As Blase and Blase found, "Conflict is inevitable . . . and considered normal, and even necessary, for organizational change and improvement" (1994, p. 24). If we work with others openly and authentically, we inevitably discover the need to be more tolerant, or more patient, or more flexible, or more receptive, or less judgmental—the list goes on and on! In short, collaboration often makes us confront just those aspects of ourselves where we most need to grow.

If your vision of what your pair or group should do differs markedly from your partner's or colleagues', you can begin to feel that others are blocking your efforts or that your own desires are getting in others' way. In such instances, a flurry of things can happen. Obstacles and blockades loom before you, you suddenly feel more tired, you blame others for not agreeing with you or being as committed as you are, or you take all the responsibility on yourself and wish you were a more cooperative person. You question whether the time and effort are worth it. In short, your own commitment to collaboration can weaken, and your attitude can shake the resolve of your colleagues to make it work. These feelings can create a downward spiral for you all.

Be on the lookout for frustrations arising from differences among you so you can bring them to the surface and discuss and resolve them before they become major conflicts. We encourage you to talk about these feelings to understand better the differences of philosophy, style, and personality that create them. Straight talk and regular feedback can keep conflicts from flaring and help you take responsibility for acknowledging and capitalizing on your differences.

We have a special recommendation in this respect: During the contracting phase, *pay extra attention to the ground rules* you set for addressing differences, and *stick to them* throughout your work together. Remember that the differences among you are your group's strengths as long as you all harness and manage them positively for the good of the work. Your ground rules help you talk about your differences of opinion, style, and philosophy so that you can accommodate these differences in the ways you work together.

Obstacles of Personal Energy

Busy teachers, counselors, principals, and school staff do exhausting work. You are with children or working on complex student problems at school from 7:30 to 3:00 with few breaks. In the late afternoon or evenings, you are evaluating student work, planning tomorrow's activities, coaching, attending meetings, or holding down a second job. The routine work itself probably leaves you feeling depleted at times. It is only natural to want to pull back, divesting yourself of commitments that seem extraordinary and limiting yourself to your own individual responsibilities.

As you consider these dilemmas of personal energy, we suggest three things:

1. Acknowledge these feelings, and above all, do not apologize for them because you feel they might undercut your collaborators. Dedicated educators are often overextended!

2. In your contracting discussions, include the topic of "overload" or "burnout," and build into your working relationships some safety valves that allow you to vary your involvement with one

another. As you move ahead to compose activities and follow through with action, level with one another about the amounts of time and energy you have to give to your work together. Agree that you will take on tasks only insomuch as you collectively and individually feel able to take them on and still carry out your other professional and personal obligations.

3. Agree with one another that part of your purpose as a collaborative pair or team is to renew one another's excitement and energy as you work together. Roland Barth described this as your "replenishing" as opposed to your "depletion" (personal communication, 1995). He argued, as we do, that collaboration is not truly beneficial to students unless it is more personally and professionally rewarding to you than working alone is. We urge you to make "replenishing" a part of your purpose as a pair or team. Build it into your ground rules. Devote time to individual needs and concerns, celebrating what you are doing well and laughing and being together.

Obstacles of Personal Commitment

At the foundation of every working relationship is each member's commitment to make that relationship work. You and your colleagues individually make that commitment, each for your own reasons. It is perfectly normal to revisit those reasons, especially when you feel your commitment flagging. This may happen because events change in your personal life or because your professional goals shift and the original commitment you made no longer has the importance it once did. In such instances, it is vital to recognize the shift in yourself and bring it to your partner's or the group's attention. In this way, your initial contract to practice straight talk with each other helps you in the tough spots—even if you resolve the issue by leaving the group.

We have stressed the importance during the convening phase of sharing honestly your individual reasons for joining together. As you reconvene in the early fall, and again as you complete an annual cycle in the spring, we encourage authentic conversation about your commitment to the pair or group. Although this may be difficult when you have been *assigned* to a group, such as a task group or the faculty, it is nevertheless a responsibility all members have to themselves and the group. Otherwise, the best result is merely the pretense of collaboration.

Often, reviewing commitments involves the whole group in rethinking its mission and relationships, perhaps to make it more rewarding for members who are feeling marginally committed. Just as often, members who are feeling new commitments to other goals and people can withdraw from the pair or group openly and positively without feeling that they have let their colleagues down. If your school is going to support collaborative relationships, all members of pairs and groups need to exercise their individual choice about committing time and energy to a form of collaboration that is meaningful to them and to their professional goals.

Nurturing the Conditions for Collaboration

We close this book by considering four factors that greatly affect your ability to work together: space, time, leadership, and culture. By doing so, we hope to help you and your colleagues discover creative ways to sustain collaboration in your school.

Collective Space

We recognize, as many others do, that school space is structured so that adults work largely isolated from one another. It is difficult to find spaces in most schools where teams of adults can assemble, work on their joint tasks, and leave their work until the next time they assemble. It is just as hard for a pair or a committee to find a meeting place that is not cluttered with the day's work with children and with furniture two sizes too small. Most schools do not even have a space in which the whole faculty can gather comfortably for discussion and small-group working sessions.

The spaces that collaboration requires need not be enormous or expensively appointed. As you move toward more consciously structuring your school space for collaboration, you might keep these goals in mind:

- Find spaces away from the bustle of the school where adults can have thoughtful exchange and professional privacy.
- Keep professional work areas separate from faculty lounges and lunchrooms designated primarily for socializing.

- Set aside rooms spacious enough to permit you to use them flexibly—sometimes to draw chairs into circles or around conference tables and sometimes for whole group meetings or small-group sessions, perhaps separated by portable partitions.
- Provide secure locations for a team's, a pair's, or a committee's working materials and papers, a place that says, "This group's work together is important enough to have its own space."
- Seek conference space and office space that you and other groups can use around the clock; do not rule out meeting spaces at central office, municipal facilities, libraries, and commercial conference locations.

You will most likely need to advocate aggressively for spaces that support your collaboration. Schools recently constructed include teacher work areas and team planning rooms, reflecting the spreading belief that "collaborative activity can enhance teachers' technical competence" (Newmann & Wehlage, 1995, p. 31). Our book can help you make your case.

Time, Time, Time

We hear from educators how importantly time, even more than space, shapes their ability to collaborate. Again, you face the double-bind of working in an institution organized for student learning, not for adult work. If the time is not identified in your schedule, the opportunity for pairs and groups to meet, work, and succeed is minimal. Linda Darling-Hammond found that "over time in the U.S., [schools] have *reduced* investments in the actual activities of teaching and learning, and in professional development for teachers, . . . [and] a vicious cycle [has been] created" (1994, p. 17, emphasis added). She calls for "greater time for collaborative work" to resolve this downward slide (p. 17).

Indeed, schools are beginning to plan time to fulfill the professional needs of adults. At the heart of many innovations is a master schedule that designates predictable blocks of time for pairs, teams, self-initiating groups, committees, and the faculty to fulfill their purposes. We suggest three principles to guide your efforts in this respect:

1. For pairs, teams, and groups that are working together daily with children, *daily planning and reflecting time is essential.* Do not proceed without it!

2. For groups whose major function is planning, policy making, or some other form of governance, time before or after school is often sufficient.

3. Blocks of intensive work time are often more productive than are short meetings; teams, task committees, standing committees, and professional development activities require such blocks. Retreats, in-service days, weekends, extended calendars, and summer (with pay) are frequently the only options for this kind of time.

Above all, make your time together productive time. As our book has repeatedly emphasized, successful collaboration depends on *people willingly committing their time to a task and to colleagues they value.* This means that your school leaders cannot design your time together any more than they can design your work and your relationships. Administrators, if they truly want faculty participation in planning and decision making, must honor the choices that collaborating adults make. Pairs and groups must have the flexibility to choose times for *their* purposes and to use that time to reach *their* goals. Members must be able to be present, both physically and emotionally, so that the time is collaboratively productive. For student-centered schools to succeed, time for staff collaboration is essential.

Leadership

Throughout our book, we have returned to the important role played by administrators and teacher leaders in nurturing collaboration. In schools structured for solitary work, leaders must generate energy and direction toward collaborative relationships. Everywhere, school leaders have a special obligation to break new paths that encourage teachers, counselors, staff, and parents to work together. We suggest that leaders focus especially on three aspects of their roles.

The first is *embodying and articulating a vision of collaboration.* Principals and lead teachers who value and are skilled in collaboration engage others in it naturally by modeling it (Blase & Blase, 1994). They consult with individual teachers, counselors, and staff—in effect, pairing with others. They form teams around immediate tasks and are accomplished facilitators of committees, managing to balance open, supportive relationships with a sustained focus on task accomplishment. Their own strong professional relationships stimulate other adults in the school to seek solutions collaboratively to the issues facing them. Such leaders articulate their own belief in collaboration and make it a primary part of the school's language.

The second aspect is *sharing power and responsibility*. Seymour Sarason, along with many others, found that teachers feel little responsibility for school-wide matters and that this attitude detracts from their effectiveness: "At the same time that [teachers] accepted responsibility for what happened in their classrooms, discharging that responsibility was negatively affected by their powerlessness in educational decision making" (1991, p. 60). School leaders—both principals and teachers—can reverse this situation by sharing power and responsibility for school-wide matters that affect classroom success.

Teacher leaders and committees of teachers can exercise choices about instructional goals, policies, practices, and professional development. Department chairs, lead teachers, and team leaders need to facilitate important decisions about curriculum, teaching methods, schedules, and student grouping. Although principals often make final decisions about school-wide schedules, space, and other resources, everyone must be involved in thinking through these decisions and must be informed about them. Everywhere, school leaders can break down old divisions between grade levels, departments, teachers' association and administration, and old and new faculty members by sharing responsibility for improving practices that all agree are below par. In lieu of a school where adults feel power and responsibility only for their individual *parts,* leaders can build a school where all adults feel power and responsibility for the *whole.*

The third aspect of the leader's role is *establishing supportive personnel policies.* Personnel policies dealing with hiring, performance evaluation, and rewards and incentives significantly influence every educator's ability to collaborate. You can revise the hiring and performance evaluation processes to embody collaborative principles rather than encouraging isolated individual performance. The results can be striking: The school begins to select new educators partly on the basis of their interest and skills in working with others, and current faculty members who venture into collaboration are rewarded for their efforts.

Changing these systems is not easy, however, and requires a good deal of school- and district-wide discussion. Leaders among both faculty and administration need to begin this dialogue among themselves, reach consensus, and then together extend it to others. Newmann and Wehlage (1995, p. 30) in their study of successful school restructuring, found that agreement on collaborative principles such as these is vital to success:

- All staff agree on one set of purposes for all students' learning.
- All staff engage in collaborative activity to achieve the purpose.
- All staff take collective responsibility for assessing and improving student learning.

By working toward agreement on these or similar principles and embedding them in the personnel systems, you can align the school's actions with its stated beliefs.

As you go about your work as a leader, we hope you will draw on chapters of our book appropriate to the kind of group you are helping to lead. Most educators—and educational leaders—have little formal education in group facilitation or collaboration. Although our book is intended to help you understand the dynamics of working relationships, it cannot prepare you to foster them (without a lot of trial and error on your part, at least!). To respond to this important challenge, consider organizational consultants, institutes on group facilitation, and workshops for teams that incorporate team-building activities. Experiment with the role of an internal consultant—a faculty member whose duties include helping pairs, teams, and groups with advice and consultation.

Leaders carry an overarching responsibility for moving the school ahead while keeping "the team" intact. Many principals and lead teachers find, however, that the first half of this challenge—the "task" dimension of their work—dominates their consciousness and activity. The second half—keeping working relationships strong—is often neglected. Few things could be more dangerous to the cause of school improvement. As a leader, you must not forget the lesson of the past half-century of leadership study: that successful organizations move ahead by constantly interweaving the woof of task orientation and the warp of relationship building. Our chapters have emphasized roles and skills that affect the quality of relationships in (and thus the productivity of) your working pairs and groups. It is up to you to help make these activities a permanent part of how you do things at your school.

A Collaborative Culture

Although the previous section highlights leaders' responsibilities, every adult in your school shares a responsibility for making your school a professional community. As Roland Barth is fond of saying, "We're all learners here; every school is a community of learners and leaders" (personal communication, 1995). As we have toured through the types of collaboration in this book and described how convening, contracting, composing, and following through can guide you, we have reiterated the importance of every member's participation in collaboration.

The culture of your school consists of the patterns of work and relationships that you have formed together. These patterns of behavior are shaped significantly by your beliefs and attitudes and those of your colleagues and leaders. In many schools, the expectation that you will share the challenges of your work with one another and help one another meet them is not a norm. Seymour Sarason (1991) argued that school reform will continue to fail so long as most schools are dominated by norms of autonomy and isolation. Fullan and Hargreaves (1991) and Judith Warren Little (1982) translated into the school setting what high-performing private companies discovered over a dozen years ago: Beliefs and behaviors built around collaborative norms—in which teachers, principals, and others explore together creative solutions to educational problems, depend on one another, and celebrate their joint accomplishments—lead to higher educational outcomes for students. As important, these are schools where dedicated professionals choose to work and are fulfilled by their work.

Because your school's culture is the product of every person's beliefs and behaviors, changing it is your business. A key to effecting change is letting go of assumptions that "things can't change," finding colleagues who share your values, and choosing a vision that springs from your common purpose. Think of the challenge as "evolving" a transformed culture through small, daily resolutions and actions. Begin by talking about forming teams and pairing up in response to challenges you and your colleagues face. Stop by a colleague's room and share one of your challenges, or inquire about his or hers. Before your next committee or team meeting, refresh your bedrock skills and your understanding of where your group is in relation to the four phases we have introduced. Speak up in the meeting if you see ways to facilitate the group's progress—drawing out a silent member, identifying a frustration or a conflict, going back to ground rules, and using a technique such as visioning or brainstorming to move the group ahead.

Taking these seemingly small steps toward new ways of working together will edge your school toward being a more collaborative place. Your footprints are as important as any others on this path. We imagine that you have read our book because you feel a need for and believe in collaborative work. What is left is for you to begin (or continue!) acting on that need and that belief. Our primer, we hope, has pointed your feet along this path, showing you where and how you might step to help you and your colleagues make your collaboration pay off.

Keep in mind, however, as you stride off down that path, that you are not setting out alone. The new, more collaborative culture of your school can only evolve collaboratively! We have written our book for you to use *with* your colleagues, as a guide for you together to grow more productive working relationships and a more collaborative culture. If you have not already done so, share this book—or the parts you have found most relevant—with a colleague or two. Then make time and find a space to have a conversation about how you, together, will begin moving yourselves—and your school—down that path.

References

Blase, J., & Blase, J. R. (1994). *Empowering teachers: What successful principals do.* Thousand Oaks, CA: Corwin.

Block, P. (1993). *Stewardship.* San Francisco: Berrett-Koehler.

Cooper, M. (1988). Whose culture is it, anyway? In A. Lieberman (Ed.), *Building a professional culture in schools* (pp. 45-54). New York: Teachers College Press.

Darling-Hammond, L. (1994). *The current status of teaching and teacher development in the United States: Background paper prepared for the National Commission on Teaching and America's future.* New York: Teachers College, Columbia University.

Fisher, R., Kopelman, E., & Kupfer Schneider, A. (1994). *Beyond Machiavelli: Tools for coping with conflict.* Cambridge, MA: Harvard University Press.

Friend, M., & Cook, L. (1992). *Interactions: Collaboration skills for school professionals.* New York: Longman.

Fullan, M., & Hargreaves, A. (1991). *What's worth fighting for: Working together for your school.* Andover, MA: Regional Laboratory for the Educational Improvement of the Northeast and Islands.

Little, J. W. (1982). Norms of collegiality and experimentation. *American Educational Research Journal, 19,* 329-338.

Maurer, R. (1991). *Managing conflict: Techniques for school administrators.* Boston: Allyn & Bacon.

Newmann, F., & Wehlage, G. (1995). *Successful school restructuring: A report to the public and educators.* Madison: University of Wisconsin, Center on Organization and Restructuring of Schools.

Noddings, N. (1984). *Caring: A feminine approach to ethics and moral education.* Berkeley: University of California Press.

Rost, J. C. (1991). *Leadership for the twenty-first century.* New York: Praeger.

Saphier, J., & King, M. (1985). Good seeds grow in strong cultures. *Educational Leadership, 43*(7), 67-74.

Sarason, S. (1991). *The predictable failure of educational reform: Can we change course before it's too late?* San Francisco: Jossey-Bass.

Index

CORWIN
PRESS

The Corwin Press logo—a raven striding across an open book—represents the happy union of courage and learning. We are a professional-level publisher of books and journals for K-12 educators, and we are committed to creating and providing resources that embody these qualities. Corwin's motto is "Success for All Learners."

$34.95